15 MINUTE

JAPANESE

LEARN IN JUST 12 WEEKS

T0333011

Mitsuko Maeda-Nye
Shizuyo Okada

REVISED EDITION
DK LONDON
Senior Editor Ankita Awasthi Tröger
Senior Art Editor Clare Shedden
Illustrators Dan Crisp, Gus Scott
Managing Editor Carine Tracanelli
Managing Art Editor Anna Hall
Production Editor Robert Dunn
Senior Production Controller Poppy David
Jacket Design Development Manager Sophia MTT
Art Director Karen Self
Associate Publishing Director Liz Wheeler
Publishing Director Jonathan Metcalf

DK DELHI
Senior Art Editors Pooja Pipil, Anjali Sachar
Editor Ekta Chadha
Art Editor Aarushi Dhawan
Assistant Editor Aashline R Avarachan
Assistant Art Editors Medha Ghosh, Mitravinda V K
Deputy Managing Editor Dharini Ganesh
Senior Managing Editor Rohan Sinha
Managing Art Editor Sudakshina Basu
Senior Jacket Designer Suhita Dharamjit
Senior Jackets Coordinator Priyanka Sharma Saddi
DTP Coordinator Vishal Bhatia
DTP Designers Rakesh Kumar, Vikram Singh,
Anita Yadav
Hi-res Coordinator Neeraj Bhatia
Production Manager Pankaj Sharma
Pre-production Manager Balwant Singh
Senior Picture Researcher Sumedha Chopra
Assistant Picture Researchers Geetam Biswas,
Shubhdeep Kaur
Picture Research Manager Taiyaba Khatoon
Creative Head Malavika Talukder

**Language content for Dorling Kindersley
by g-and-w publishing
Additional translations for 2024 edition
by Andiamo! Language Services Ltd**

This edition published in 2024
First published in Great Britain in 2005 by
Dorling Kindersley Limited
DK, 20 Vauxhall Bridge Road, London SW1V 2SA

The authorised representative in the EEA is
Dorling Kindersley Verlag GmbH. Arnulfstr. 124,
80636 Munich, Germany

Copyright © 2005, 2013, 2019, 2024
Dorling Kindersley Limited
A Penguin Random House Company
10 9 8 7 6 5 4
005–336544–Jan/2024

A CIP catalogue record for this book
is available from the British Library.
ISBN 978-0-2416-3163-8

Printed and bound in China

www.dk.com

Contents

How to use this book

Twelve themed chapters are broken down into five daily 15-minute lessons, allowing you to work through four teaching units and one revision unit each week. The lessons cover a range of practical themes, including leisure, business, food and drink, and travel. A reference section at the end contains a menu guide, an English-to-Japanese dictionary, and a guide to the Japanese writing system.

Warm up
Each day starts with a warm up that encourages you to recall vocabulary or phrases you have learned previously.

Instructions
Each exercise is numbered and introduced by instructions that explain what to do. In some cases additional information is given about the language point being covered.

Text styles
Japanese script and easy-to-read pronunciation are shown, along with the English translation.

Audio
This icon indicates that you should listen to audio recordings in order to do the exercise. See page 7 for details of how to access and use the audio app.

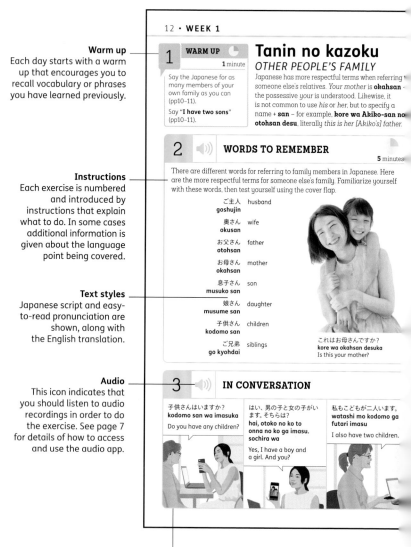

12 · WEEK 1

1 **WARM UP** 1 minute

Say the Japanese for as many members of your own family as you can (pp10–11).

Say "**I have two sons**" (pp10–11).

Tanin no kazoku
OTHER PEOPLE'S FAMILY

Japanese has more respectful terms when referring to someone else's relatives. *Your mother* is **okahsan** – the possessive *your* is understood. Likewise, it is not common to use *his* or *her*, but to specify a name + **san** – for example, **kore wa Akiko-san no otohsan desu**, literally *this is her [Akiko's] father.*

2 **WORDS TO REMEMBER** 5 minutes

There are different words for referring to family members in Japanese. Here are the more respectful terms for someone else's family. Familiarize yourself with these words, then test yourself using the cover flap.

ご主人 **goshujin**	husband
奥さん **okusan**	wife
お父さん **otohsan**	father
お母さん **okahsan**	mother
息子さん **musuko san**	son
娘さん **musume san**	daughter
子供さん **kodomo san**	children
ご兄弟 **go kyohdai**	siblings

これはお母さんですか?
kore wa okahsan desuka
Is this your mother?

3 **IN CONVERSATION**

子供さんはいますか?
kodomo san wa imasuka
Do you have any children?

はい、男の子と女の子がいます。そちらは?
hai, otoko no ko to onna no ko ga imasu. sochira wa
Yes, I have a boy and a girl. And you?

私もこどもが二人います。
watashi mo kodomo ga futari imasu
I also have two children.

In conversation
Illustrated dialogues reflecting how vocabulary and phrases are used in everyday situations appear throughout the book.

Learn
Keep the flaps
open while
you learn.

Revise
Use the flaps to
cover the answers
when you are ready
to test yourself.

INTRODUCTIONS · 13

Conversational tip Forming a question in Japanese is straightforward. Generally
you add the marker or particle か **ka** (p158) to the end of a sentence – for example,
a-re wa musuko san desu (*that's your son*) becomes **a-re wa musuko san desuka**
(*is that your son?*). In less formal spoken Japanese, **ka** is sometimes dropped –
a-re wa musuko san – but an upward tone at the end indicates it is a question.

Cultural/Conversational tip
These panels provide
additional insights into
life in Japan and
language usage.

4 USEFUL PHRASES

3 minutes

Learn these phrases, then test yourself using the cover flap.

| | Do you have any siblings? (formal) | ご兄弟はいらっしゃいますか？ **go kyohdai wa irasshai masuka** |
| | Do you have any siblings? (informal) | 兄弟はいるの？ **kyohdai wa iruno** |

| | Is this your father? | これはお父さんですか？ **kore wa otohsan desuka** |
| | Is that your son? (formal) | あれは息子さんですか？ **a-re wa musuko san desuka** |

| | This is Akiko's daughter. | これは明子さんの娘さんです。 **kore wa akiko-san no musume san desu** |
| | Is that your little sister? (informal) | あれは妹さん？ **a-re wa imohto san** |

Exercises
Familiarizing you with
terms relevant to each topic,
these help you build your
vocabulary, learn useful
phrases, connect words
to visuals, and practice
what you learn.

4 minutes

は娘と息子です。
e wa musume to
suko desu

is my daughter
son.

5 SAY IT

2 minutes

Is this your wife?
Is that your
little brother?
Do you have a
son? (informal)
This is Akiko's
mother.

Time yourself
This icon and text to the
right of the heading show
you how long you need to
spend on each exercise.

Say it
In these exercises you are asked
to apply what you have learned
using different vocabulary.

»

Revision

At the end of every week's lessons, a revision unit lets you test yourself on what you have learnt so far. A recap of selected elements from previous lessons helps to reinforce your knowledge.

Test yourself
Use the cover flap to conceal the answers while you revise.

Reference

This section appears at the end of the book, and brings together all the words and phrases you have learnt over the weeks. While the menu guide focuses on food and drink, the dictionary lists Japanese translations of common words and phrases.

Dictionaries
A mini-dictionary provides ready reference from English to Japanese for 2,000 words.

Menu guide
Use this guide as a reference for food terminology and popular Japanese dishes.

LANGUAGE AND PRONUNCIATION GUIDE

Different levels of formality are inbuilt into the Japanese language and it takes time to acquire a feel for this. The lessons in this book will introduce you to polite, but not overformal, Japanese.

Most Japanese sounds will already be familiar to you, and the pronunciation guide given for all words and phrases in *15 Minute Japanese* is designed to be natural to read. However, a few sounds require additional explanation:

r	a Japanese r is pronounced like a cross between an English *r* and *l*
ih	*ee* as in *sheep*
eh	long *eh*, like a longer version of the sound in *they*
oh	long *o* as in *motor*
u-	long *u* as in *spoon*
final u	the final *u* written on the end of words such as **desu** (*is/are*) and (**ga/wa**) **arimasu** (*there is/are*) is only slightly pronounced and often sounds more like a double letter (for example, *dess*).

The Japanese language is based on syllables, rather than individual letters. Each syllable is pronounced with roughly equal stress.

HOW TO USE THE AUDIO APP

The free audio app accompanying this book contains audio recordings for all numbered exercises on the teaching pages, except for the Warm Up and Say It exercises (look out for the audio icon). There is no audio for the revision pages.

To start using the audio with this book, download the **DK 15 Minute Language Course** app on your tablet or smartphone from the App Store or Google Play and select your book from the list of available titles. Please note that this app is not a stand-alone course, but is designed to be used together with the book to familiarize you with the language and provide examples for you to repeat aloud.

There are two ways in which you can use the audio. The first is to read through the 15-minute lessons using just the book, then go back and work with the audio and the book together. Or you can combine the book and the audio from the start, pausing the app to read the instructions on the page.

You are encouraged to listen to the audio and repeat the words and sentences out loud until you are confident you understand and can pronounce what has been said. Remember that repetition is vital for language learning. The more often you listen to a conversation or repeat an oral exercise, the more the new language will sink in.

SUPPORTING AUDIO
This icon indicates that audio recordings are available for you to listen to.

FREE AUDIO APP

Konnichiwa
HELLO

The Japanese bow is famous: the lower the bow, the more respectful. Traditionally, there would not be any contact in the form of handshakes or kisses, but this is now changing. Shaking hands, sometimes bowing at the same time, has become a more common form of greeting in business and social situations, especially when meeting foreigners.

1 WARM UP
1 minute

The Warm Up panel appears at the beginning of each topic. Use it to reinforce what you have already learned and to prepare yourself for moving ahead with the new subject.

2 WORDS TO REMEMBER
2 minutes

Familiarize yourself with these words by reading them aloud several times, then test yourself by concealing the Japanese on the left with the cover flap.

おはようございます **ohayoh gozaimasu**	Good morning
こんばんは **konbanwa**	Good evening
さようなら **sayohnara**	Goodbye (formal)
さよなら **sayonara**	Goodbye (informal)
ありがとう／ありが とうございます **arigatoh/arigatoh gozaimasu**	Thank you/ Thank you very much

こんにちは。
konnichiwa
Hello!

3 IN CONVERSATION: FORMAL
3 minutes

こんにちは。
私の名前は岡田です。
konnichiwa. watashi no namae wa okada desu

Hello. My name is Okada.

こんにちは。私の名前は
ロバート・パーカーです。
konnichiwa. watashi no namae wa robahto bahkah desu

Hello. My name is Robert Barker.

どうぞ、よろしく。
dohzo yoroshiku

Pleased to meet you.

4 PUT INTO PRACTICE

3 minutes

Read the Japanese on the left and follow the instructions to complete this dialogue. Then test yourself by concealing the Japanese on the right with the cover flap.

こんばんは。
konbanwa
Good evening.
Say: Good evening.

こんばんは。
konbanwa

私の名前は
前田美樹郎です。
watashi no namae wa maeda mikiro desu
My name is Maeda Mikiro.
Say: Pleased to meet you, Maeda-san.

どうぞ、よろ
しく前田さん。
dohzo yoroshiku maeda-san

Conversational tip

The Japanese introduce themselves using either just the family name – Okada – or the family name, then the first name – Maeda Mikiro. But they are used to hearing Western names the other way – Robert Barker. Avoid asking someone their name directly; instead, listen carefully to all the introductions. When talking to/about others, you should add the honorific **san**, but don't use it when talking about yourself.

5 USEFUL PHRASES

3 minutes

Learn these phrases by reading them aloud several times, then test yourself by concealing the Japanese on the right with the cover flap.

My name is...
私の名前は... です。
watashi no namae wa... desu

Pleased to meet you.
どうぞ、よろしく。
dohzo yoroshiku

See you soon/
See you tomorrow.
ではまた／ではまたあした。
dewa mata/dewa mata ashita

6 IN CONVERSATION: INFORMAL

3 minutes

ではまたあした?
dewa mata ashita

See you tomorrow?

はい、ではまたあした。
hai, dewa mata ashita

Yes, see you tomorrow.

さよなら。
sayonara

Goodbye.

Watashi no kazoku
MY FAMILY

Say "**hello**" and "**goodbye**" in Japanese (pp8–9).

Now say "**My name is...**" (pp8–9).

Say "**Pleased to meet you**" (pp8–9).

Japanese has two sets of vocabulary for family members, depending on whether you are talking about your own or someone else's. This lesson talks about your own family. As Japanese words for family relationships include the possessive – for example, **chichi** means *my father*, **musume** means *my daughter*, etc – there is no need for a separate word meaning *my*.

2 **MATCH AND REPEAT**

5 minutes

Look at the people in this scene and match their numbers to the vocabulary list on the left. Then test yourself by concealing the Japanese on the left using the cover flap.

❶ 祖母
 sobo

❷ 父
 chichi

❸ 母
 haha

❹ 祖父
 sofu

❺ 息子
 musuko

❻ 娘
 musume

❶ my grandmother

❷ my father

❸ my mother

❹ my grandfather

❺ my son

❻ my daughter

Conversational tip Alongside terms for individual family members, Japanese also has collective nouns for some relationships. Grandparents are **sofubo**, while parents are **ryoshin**. The word **kyodai** is used for siblings: **kyohdal ga yo nln lmasu** (*I have four siblings*).

3 WORDS TO REMEMBER:
RELATIVES

5 minutes

Familiarize yourself with these words, then test yourself using the cover flap. Note that Japanese distinguishes between little and big sister/brother.

夫
otto
my husband

妻
tsuma
my wife

my big sister/ my little sister	姉／妹 **ane/imohto**
my big brother/ my little brother	兄／弟 **ani/otohto**
my siblings	兄弟 **kyohdai**
my uncle/ my aunt	おじ／おば **oji/oba**
I'm married.	結婚しています。 **kekkon shite imasu**
I have four children.	子供が四人います。 **kodomo ga yo nin imasu**
We have two daughters.	娘が二人います。 **musume ga futari imasu**

これは私の妻です。
kore wa watashi no tsuma desu
This is my wife.

4 WORDS TO REMEMBER:
NUMBERS

4 minutes

The general numbers opposite are used for mathematical functions or for money. The Japanese also use classifiers, such as the ones below, to count specific things. These vary with the nature of what is being counted – for example, its shape. A beginner can get away with using the general numbers, but it's useful to know the classifiers used for people to talk about your family. Familiarize yourself with these words, then test yourself using the cover flap.

一人	**hitori**	1 person
二人	**futari**	2 people
三人	**san nin**	3 people
四人	**yo nin**	4 people
五人	**go nin**	5 people
六人	**roku nin**	6 people
七人	**shichi nin**	7 people
八人	**hachi nin**	8 people
九人	**kyu nin**	9 people
十人	**jyu nin**	10 people

one	一 **ichi**
two	二 **ni**
three	三 **san**
four	四 **shi/yon**
five	五 **go**
six	六 **roku**
seven	七 **shichi/nana**
eight	八 **hachi**
nine	九 **kyu**
ten	十 **jyu**

Tanin no kazoku
OTHER PEOPLE'S FAMILY

1 | **WARM UP** | 1 minute

Say the Japanese for as many members of your own family as you can (pp10–11).

Say "**I have two sons**" (pp10–11).

Japanese has more respectful terms when referring to someone else's relatives. *Your mother* is **okahsan** – the possessive *your* is understood. Likewise, it is not common to use *his* or *her*, but to specify a name + **san** – for example, **kore wa Akiko-san no otohsan desu**, literally *this is her [Akiko's] father.*

2 🔊 **WORDS TO REMEMBER**

5 minutes

There are different words for referring to family members in Japanese. Here are the more respectful terms for someone else's family. Familiarize yourself with these words, then test yourself using the cover flap.

ご主人 **goshujin**	husband
奥さん **okusan**	wife
お父さん **otohsan**	father
お母さん **okahsan**	mother
息子さん **musuko san**	son
娘さん **musume san**	daughter
子供さん **kodomo san**	children
ご兄弟 **go kyohdai**	siblings

これはお母さんですか？
kore wa okahsan desuka
Is this your mother?

3 🔊 **IN CONVERSATION**

子供さんはいますか？
kodomo san wa imasuka

Do you have any children?

はい、男の子と女の子がいます。そちらは？
hai, otoko no ko to onna no ko ga imasu. sochira wa

Yes, I have a boy and a girl. And you?

私もこどもが二人います。
watashi mo kodomo ga futari imasu

I also have two children.

Conversational tip Forming a question in Japanese is straightforward. Generally you add the marker or particle か **ka** (p158) to the end of a sentence – for example, **a-re wa musuko san desu** (*that's your son*) becomes **a-re wa musuko san desuka** (*is that your son?*). In less formal spoken Japanese, **ka** is sometimes dropped – **a-re wa musuko san** – but an upward tone at the end indicates it is a question.

4 USEFUL PHRASES

3 minutes

Learn these phrases, then test yourself using the cover flap.

Do you have any siblings? (formal)
ご兄弟はいらっしゃいますか？
go kyohdai wa irasshai masuka

Do you have any siblings? (informal)
兄弟はいるの？
kyohdai wa iruno

Is this your father?
これはお父さんですか？
kore wa otohsan desuka

Is that your son? (formal)
あれは息子さんですか？
a-re wa musuko san desuka

This is Akiko's daughter.
これは明子さんの娘さんです。
kore wa akiko-san no musume san desu

Is that your little sister? (informal)
あれは妹さん？
a-re wa imohto san

4 minutes

これは娘と息子です。
kore wa musume to musuko desu

This is my daughter and son.

5 SAY IT

2 minutes

Is this your wife?

Is that your little brother?

Do you have a son? (informal)

This is Akiko's mother.

1 WARM UP

1 minute

Say "**See you soon**" (pp8–9).

Say "**I am married**" (pp10–11), "**I have a son**", and "**Is this your wife?**" (pp12–13).

Desu/ga arimasu
TO BE/THERE IS

The most common Japanese verb is **desu**, meaning *is, are,* or *am*. The **u** is said only slightly, making it sound more like **dess**. **Desu** comes at the end of the sentence and does not change with the subject (*I, he, we,* etc): **watashi wa Robahto desu** (*I'm Robert*), **kare/kanojo wa isha desu** (*he/she is a doctor*), **watashi tachi wa nihonjin desu** (*we're Japanese*).

2 **DESU**: TO BE

2 minutes

The present tense of the verb uses **desu** (*be/is, am/are/is being*); the present negative is **dewa arimasen** (*don't be/is not, am not/aren't/isn't being*). The past tense uses **deshita** (*was*) or **dewa arimasen deshita** (*wasn't*). **Desu** is used at the end of sentences expressing *am/are/is* in order to make an assertive phrase sound polite. Practise the sample sentences, then test yourself using the cover flap.

明子さんは学生です。
akiko-san wa gakusei desu

Akiko is a student. (present)

私は編集者です。
watashi wa henshuhsha desu

I am an editor. (present)

私は日本人です。
watashi wa nihonjin desu

I'm Japanese. (present)

今10時です。
ima jyuji desu

It's ten o'clock. (present)

これは私のかばんではありません。
kore wa watashi no kaban dewa arimasen

This is not my bag. (present negative)

父は医者でした。
chichi wa isha deshita

My father was a doctor. (past)

昨日は休みではありませんでした。
kino wa yasumi dewa arimasen deshita

Yesterday was not a holiday. (past negative)

3 ARIMASU: THERE IS

5 minutes

An informal and straightforward way to talk about what you have is to use the expression **ga/wa** (p158) + **arimasu**, literally meaning *there is*. This changes to **ga/wa** + **imasu** when talking about people rather than objects. Practise the sample sentences, then test yourself using the cover flap.

息子には車があります。
musuko niwa kuruma ga arimasu
My son has a car.

Do you have any children?	子供さんはいますか？	**kodomo san wa imasuka**
I have three children.	子供が三人います。	**kodomo ga san nin imasu**
I have a little sister.	妹がいます。	**imohto ga imasu**
I have a business card.	名刺があります。	**meishi ga arimasu**

4 NEGATIVES

3 minutes

Negative sentences are made in different ways in Japanese, but sometimes use the negative phrase **arimasen**. Read these sentences aloud, then test yourself using the cover flap.

We're not American.	アメリカ人ではありません。	**amerika jin dewa arimasen**
I don't have a car.	私には車がありません。	**watashi niwa kuruma ga arimasen**

5 PUT INTO PRACTICE

4 minutes

Complete this dialogue, then test yourself using the cover flap.

こんばんは。
konbanwa
Good evening.
Say: Good evening.
I'm Robert.

こんばんは。私は ロバートです。
konbanwa. watashi wa robahto desu

どうぞよろしく。
dohzo yoroshiku
Pleased to meet you.
Say: This is my business card.

私の名刺です。
watashi no meishi desu

Fukushu to kurikaeshi
REVIEW AND REPEAT

How many?

❶ 三
san

❷ 九
kyu

❸ 四
shi/yon

❹ 二
ni

❺ 八
hachi

❻ 十
jyu

❼ 五
go

❽ 七
shichi/nana

❾ 六
roku

Hello

❶ こんにちは。
私の名前は...です。
konnichiwa. watashi no namae wa... desu

❷ どうぞ、よろしく
dohzo yoroshiku

❸ 息子が二人います。
子供さんはいますか？
musuko ga futari imasu. kodomo san wa imasuka

❹ さようなら
sayohnara

---

1 HOW MANY?
2 minutes

Say these numbers in Japanese, then test yourself using the cover flap.

3 ❶
9 ❷
4 ❸
2 ❹
8 ❺
10 ❻
5 ❼
7 ❾
6
❽

---

2 HELLO
4 minutes

You meet someone in a formal situation. Join in the conversation, replying in Japanese following the numbered English prompts.

konbanwa. watashi no namae wa robahto bahkah desu
❶ Hello. My name is... [your name].

kore wa watashi no tsuma desu
❷ Pleased to meet you.

kodomo san wa imasuka
❸ I have two sons. Do you have any children?

yo nin imasu
❹ Goodbye.

3 BE OR HAVE

5 minutes

Fill in the blanks with **desu** (*to be*) or **arimasu/ imasu** (*there is/are* used to mean *has/have*).

❶ watashi no namae wa okada _____ .

❷ anata wa gakusei san _____ ka.

❸ sarah-san wa igirisu jin _____ .

❹ watashi wa nihonjin _____ .

❺ meishi ga _____ .

❻ kore wa watashi no otto _____ .

❼ musume ga futari _____ .

❽ ani ga _____ .

Be or have

❶ です
desu

❷ です
desu

❸ です
desu

❹ です
desu

❺ あります
arimasu

❻ です
desu

❼ います
imasu

❽ います
imasu

4 FAMILY

4 minutes

Name these family members in Japanese.

❶ my grandmother

my grandfather ❻

❸ my father   ❹ my mother

my son ❷   ❺ my daughter

Family

❶ 祖母
sobo

❷ 息子
musuko

❸ 父
chichi

❹ 母
haha

❺ 娘
musume

❻ 祖父
sofu

Kafe de
IN THE CAFÉ

1 | **WARM UP** | 1 minute

Count to ten (pp10–11).

Remind yourself how to say "**hello**" and "**goodbye**" (pp8–9).

Ask "**Do you have a car?**" (pp14–15).

You will find a range of cafés in Japan. **Chaya** or **chamise** are traditional Japanese teahouses, while **amamidokoro** offer Japanese sweets accompanied by green tea. Western-style cafés, simply called **kafe** or **kissaten**, are also very popular, especially amongst younger Japanese. Both counter service and table service are common, and tipping is rare.

2 **WORDS TO REMEMBER**

Familiarize yourself with these words, then test yourself using the cover flap.

サンドイッチ **sando icchi**	sandwich
ココア **kokoa**	hot chocolate
ブラックコーヒー **burakku koh-hi**	black coffee
紅茶 **kohcha**	black tea (literally *red tea*)
ミルクティー **miruku tih**	tea with milk
お茶 **ocha** (green) tea	

砂糖
satoh
sugar

コーヒー
koh-hi
coffee

3 **IN CONVERSATION**

コーヒーをお願いします。
koh-hi o onegai shimasu
A coffee, please.

他にご注文は？
hoka ni gochumon wa
Anything else?

ケーキはありますか？
kehki wa arimasuka
Do you have any cakes?

Cultural tip The generic Japanese word for tea is **cha/ocha**. Japanese green tea, **ryokucha**, and varieties of it such as **sencha**, are offered in **amamidokoro** or during/after meals in restaurants. Western-style tea is known as **kohcha** (literally *red tea*).

5 minutes

ケーキ
kehki
cake

Learn these phrases, then test yourself using the cover flap.

ブラックコーヒーをお願いします。
burakku koh-hi o onegai shimasu

A black coffee, please.

他にご注文は？
hoka ni gochumon wa

Anything else?

ケーキもお願いします。
kehki mo onegai shimasu

A cake, too, please.

いくらですか？
ikura desuka

How much is that?

4 minutes

はい、ございます。
hai, gozaimasu

Yes, certainly.

じゃケーキをお願いします。いくらですか？
jya kehki o onegai shimasu. ikura desuka

Then I'd like a cake, please. How much is that?

1,300円です。
sen sanbyaku en desu

That's 1,300 yen.

1 WARM UP
1 minute

Say "**A coffee, please**" (pp18–19).

Say "**I don't have a brother**" (pp14–15).

Ask "**Do you have any cakes?**" (pp18–19).

Resutoran de
IN THE RESTAURANT

There are a variety of eating places in Japan, including **yatai** (*street stalls*), **kicchin cah** (*food trucks*), **izakaya** (*informal pubs*), and **kafe** (pp18–19). **Ryohtei** are high-end restaurants that serve traditional Japanese cuisine in private rooms. Department stores often house relaxed **resutoran** on the upper floors, open until about 10pm and serving both international and Japanese dishes.

2 🔊 MATCH AND REPEAT
5 minutes

Match the numbered items to the list, then test yourself using the cover flap.

❶ グラス
gurasu

❷ 茶碗
chawan

❸ おはし
ohashi

❹ フォーク
fohku

❺ ナイフ
naifu

❻ スプーン
supuun

❼ おしぼり
oshibori

❽ お皿
osara

❷ bowl

❸ chopsticks

glass ❶

❹ fork

❺ knife

❻ spoon

hand towel ❼

❽ plate

3 🔊 IN CONVERSATION

四人用のテーブルは空いていますか?
yonin yoh no tehburu wa aite imasuka

Do you have a table for four?

予約なさっていますか?
yoyaku nasatte imasuka

Do you have a reservation?

はい、バーカーで予約しています。
hai, bahkah de yoyaku shite imasu

Yes, in the name of Barker.

4 WORDS TO REMEMBER

3 minutes

Familiarize yourself with these words, then test yourself using the cover flap.

menu	メニュー **menyu**
wine list	ワインリスト **wain risuto**
starters	前菜 **zen sai**
main courses	メインコース **mein kohsu**
desserts	デザート **dezahto**
breakfast	朝食 **chohshoku**
lunch	昼食 **chu-shoku**
dinner	夕食 **yu-shoku**

家族と昼食を食べています。
kazoku to chu-shoku o tabete imasu
I'm having lunch with my family.

5 USEFUL PHRASES

2 minutes

Learn these phrases, then test yourself using the cover flap.

What type of sushi do you have?	どんなお寿司 があ りますか？ **don-na osushi ga arimasuka**
Where can I pay?	どこで払えますか？ **doko de harae masuka**

4 minutes

席はどこがよろしい ですか？
seki wa doko ga yoroshii desuka

Where would you like to sit?

窓際の席をお願いします。
madogiwa no seki o onegai shimasu

Near a window, please.

はい。こちらへどうぞ。
hai. kochira e dohzo

Very well. Here you are.

Tabemono
DISHES

1 **WARM UP**
1 minute

Say "**I'm Japanese**" (pp10–11) and "**Are you an editor?**" (pp14–15).

Ask "**Do you have a fork?**" (pp20–21).

Say "**A sandwich, please**" (pp18–19).

Japan is famous for its **sushi** and fermented foods such as **miso** (*fermented soyabean paste*), **shoyu** (*soy sauce*), and **tsukemono** (*pickles*). A typical meal would consist of rice, miso soup, and a variety of fish, meat, and vegetable dishes, usually served with pickles and condiments such as ginger and horseradish. Dessert can be sweet puddings such as **kanten** (*Japanese jelly*) and, sometimes, fruit.

2 🔊 **MATCH AND REPEAT**

4 minutes

Match the numbered items to the list, then test yourself using the cover flap.

❶ 果物
kudamono

❷ きのこ
kinoko

❸ 米
kome

❹ 野菜
yasai

❺ 麺類
men rui

❻ スープ
supu

❼ 魚
sakana

❽ シーフード
shihfu-do

❾ 肉
niku

❶ fruit
❷ mushrooms
❸ rice
❹ vegetables
❺ noodles
❻ soup
❼ fish
❽ seafood
❾ meat

Cultural tip In restaurants and food halls, **teishoku** (*set menus*) are popular, particularly at lunchtime. These consist of a soup, rice, pickles, and other dishes of your choice – all presented on a tray.

3 WORDS TO REMEMBER: COOKING METHODS

3 minutes

Familiarize yourself with these words, then test yourself using the cover flap.

この魚は生ですか?
kono sakana wa nama desuka
Is this fish raw?

fried	揚げた	**ageta**
grilled	焼いた	**yaita**
roasted	ローストした	**rohsuto shita**
boiled	ゆでた	**yudeta**
simmered	煮た	**nita**
steamed	蒸した	**mushita**
raw	生の	**nama no**

4 WORDS TO REMEMBER: DRINKS

3 minutes

Familiarize yourself with these words, then test yourself using the cover flap.

お酒
osake
sake/alcoholic drinks

water	水	**mizu**
mineral water	ミネラルウォーター	**mineraru wohtah**
wine	ワイン	**wain**
beer	ビール	**bihru**
fruit juice	フルーツジュース	**furutsu jyusu**

5 USEFUL PHRASES

2 minutes

Learn these phrases, then test yourself using the cover flap.

I'm vegetarian.	ベジタリアンです。 **bejitarian desu**
I'm allergic to nuts.	ナッツ類にアレルギーがあります。 **nattsu rui ni arerugih ga arimasu**
What is "oden"?	おでんとは何ですか? **oden towa nan desuka**

6 SAY IT

2 minutes

What is "yakitori"?

I'm allergic to seafood.

A beer, please.

1 WARM UP

1 minute

What are "**breakfast**", "**lunch**", and "**dinner**" in Japanese? (pp20–21).

Say "**I'm vegetarian**" and "**What is oden?**" in Japanese (pp22–3).

Say "**He is**" (pp14–15).

Onegai shimasu
REQUESTS

The simplest way to request or ask for something in Japanese is to say what you want, followed by **(o) onegai shimasu** (*please*). You can use this in almost any situation. However, if you really want to impress the people to whom you are speaking, for example in a business situation, you could use the ultra-polite phrase **itadake masuka**.

2 BASIC REQUESTS

6 minutes

The most common way to make a request is to use **(o) onegai shimasu**, but you may also come across **onegai shimasu** used with the particle **de** – this is used to indicate the means by which an action has to be completed. Practise the sample sentences, then test yourself using the cover flap.

紅茶をお願いします。 **kohcha o onegai shimasu**	(I'd like) some tea, please.
ケーキをお願いします。 **kehki o onegai shimasu**	(I'd like) a cake, please.
フォークをお願いします。 **fohku o onegai shimasu**	(I'd like) a fork, please.
3人用のテーブル をお願いします。 **san nin yoh no tehburu o onegai shimasu**	(I'd like) a table for three, please.
メニューをお願いします。 **menyu o onegai shimasu**	(I'd like) the menu, please.
お菓子をお願いします。 **okashi o onegai shimasu**	(I'd like) some sweets, please.
コーヒーをお願いします。 **koh-hi o onegai shimasu**	(I'd like) coffee, please.
ブラックでお願いします。 **burakku de onegai shimasu**	I would like it (coffee) black, please.
カードでお願いします。 **kahdo de onegai shimasu**	(Payment) by card, please.

お餅をお願いします。
omochi o onegai shimasu
(I'd like) some mochi, please.

Conversational tip In Japanese, **onegai shimasu** is the most commonly used phrase for requests and can be used anywhere. However, if you want to see choices before buying something or can't find what you are looking for, you can say **ga hoshii no desuga** (*I would like...*) to the shop assistant.

3 POLITE REQUESTS

4 minutes

In any business or social situation where you may want to appear ultra-polite, especially when talking to someone senior, you can use the phrase **itadake masuka**. Practise the sample sentences, then test yourself using the cover flap.

Could I have some water, please?

お水をいただけますか？
omizu o itadake masuka

Could we pay separately, please?

会計を別々にして
いただけますか？
kaikei o betsubetsu ni shite itadake masuka

Could you wrap it up, please?

包んでいただけますか？
tsutsunde itadake masuka

4 PUT INTO PRACTICE

4 minutes

Complete this dialogue, then test yourself using the cover flap.

こんばんは。予約なさって
いますか？
konbanwa. yoyaku nasatte imasuka
Good evening. Do you have a reservation?

Say: No, but I'd like a table for three, please.

いいえ、でも3人用のテーブルをお願いします。
ihe, demo san nin yoh no tehburu o onegai shimasu

お飲物は何になさいますか？
onomimono wa nani ni nasai masuka
What would you like to drink?

Say: A beer, please.

ビールをお願いします。
bihru o onegai shimasu

Fukushu to kurikaeshi
REVIEW AND REPEAT

Kotae *Answers*
(Cover with flap)

At the table

❶ スープ
supu

❷ 野菜
yasai

❸ 魚
sakana

❹ 肉
niku

❺ グラス
gurasu

This is my…

❶ これは私の夫です。
kore wa watashi no otto desu

❷ これは私の娘です。
kore wa watashi no musume desu

❸ これは私の兄弟です。
kore wa watashi no kyohdai desu

I'd like…

❶ お茶をお願いします。
ocha o onegai shimasu

❷ コーヒーをお願いします。
koh-hi o onegai shimasu

❸ ケーキをお願いします。
kehki o onegai shimasu

❹ 砂糖をお願いします。
satoh o onegai shimasu

---

1   AT THE TABLE

Name these items in Japanese.

❶ soup   vegetables ❷

❸ fish

meat ❹

glass ❺

---

2   THIS IS MY…

4 minutes

Say these sentences in Japanese.

❶ This is my husband.
❷ This is my daughter.
❸ These are my siblings.

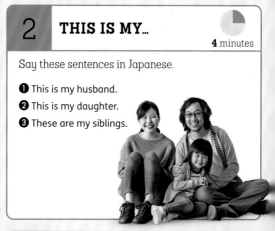

---

3   I'D LIKE…

3 minutes

Say you'd like these items in Japanese.

❶ green tea   coffee ❷   ❸ cake

sugar ❹

4 minutes

- **6** noodles
- rice **7**
- **8** chopsticks
- **9** hand towel
- **10** beer

At the table

6 麺類
men rui

7 米
kome

8 おはし
ohashi

9 おしぼり
oshibori

10 ビール
bihru

4 RESTAURANT

4 minutes

You arrive at a restaurant. Join in the conversation, replying in Japanese following the numbered English prompts.

konbanwa
1 Do you have a table for three?

yoyaku nasatte imasuka
2 Yes, in the name of Suzuki.

seki wa doko ga yoroshii desuka
3 Near a window, please.

kochira e dohzo
4 The menu, please.

hai, dohzo
5 Do you have a wine list?

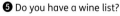

Restaurant

1 3人用のテーブルは空いていますか？
san nin yoh no tehburu wa aite imasuka

2 はい、鈴木で予約しています。
hai, suzuki de yoyaku shite imasu

3 窓際の席をお願いします。
madogiwa no seki o onegai shimasu

4 メニューをお願いします。
menyu o onegai shimasu

5 ワインリストはありますか？
wain risuto wa arimasuka

Hizuke to toshitsuki
DAYS AND MONTHS

1 WARM UP
1 minute

How do you say "**I have four children**"? (pp10–11).

Say "**We're not English**" and "**I don't have a car**" (pp14–15).

What is the Japanese for "**my mother**"? (pp10–11).

In Japanese, dates are written in the opposite order to English: **nen** (*year*), **gatsu** (*month*), **nichi** (*day of the month* or *date*), and **yohbi** (*day of the week*). The most important holiday of the year in Japan is the three-day **oshogatsu** (*new year holiday*), which the Japanese usually spend with family. Christmas is also celebrated, but this is more often spent with friends.

2 WORDS TO REMEMBER: DAYS
5 minutes

月曜日 **getsuyohbi**	Monday
火曜日 **kayohbi**	Tuesday
水曜日 **suiyohbi**	Wednesday
木曜日 **mokuyohbi**	Thursday
金曜日 **kinyohbi**	Friday
土曜日 **doyohbi**	Saturday
日曜日 **nichiyohbi**	Sunday
今日 **kyoh**	today
明日 **ashita**	tomorrow
昨日 **kinoh**	yesterday

Familiarize yourself with these words, then test yourself using the cover flap.

今日予約があります。
kyoh yoyaku ga arimasu
I have a reservation for today.

明日お会いしましょう。
ashita oai shimashoh
We meet tomorrow.

3 USEFUL PHRASES: DAYS
2 minutes

Learn these phrases, then test yourself using the cover flap.

ミーティングは火曜日ではありません。 **mihtingu wa kayoh bi dewa arimasen**	The meeting isn't on Tuesday.
日曜日に仕事をします。 **nichiyoh bi ni shigoto o shimasu**	I work on Sundays.

4 WORDS TO REMEMBER: MONTHS

5 minutes

Japanese months are named simply 1 month, 2 month, etc. When the words are used by themselves, month is **tsuki** and year is **toshi**, but when used with a specific number, month is **gatsu** and year is **nen**. Familiarize yourself with these words, then test yourself using the cover flap.

私たちの結婚記念日は七月です。
watashi tachi no kekkon kinenbi wa shichi gatsu desu
Our wedding anniversary is in July.

January	一月	**ichi gatsu**
February	二月	**ni gatsu**
March	三月	**san gatsu**
April	四月	**shi gatsu**
May	五月	**go gatsu**
June	六月	**roku gatsu**
July	七月	**shichi gatsu**
August	八月	**hachi gatsu**
September	九月	**ku gatsu**
October	十月	**jyu gatsu**
November	十一月	**jyu-ichi gatsu**
December	十二月	**jyu-ni gatsu**
next month	来月	**rai getsu**
last month	先月	**sen getsu**
month	月	**tsuki**
year	年	**toshi**

大晦日は十二月です。
oomisoka wa jyu-ni gatsu desu
New year's eve is in December.

5 USEFUL PHRASES: MONTHS

2 minutes

Learn these phrases, then test yourself using the cover flap.

| My children are on holiday in August. | 子供たちは八月は休みです。
kodomo tachi wa hachi gatsu wa yasumi desu |
| My birthday is in June. | 私の誕生日は六月です。
watashi no tanjyoh bi wa roku gatsu desu |

Jikan to suhji
TIME AND NUMBERS

1 WARM UP
1 minute

Count in Japanese from 1 to 10 (pp10–11).

Say "**Do you have a reservation?**" (pp20–21).

Say "**The meeting isn't on Wednesday**" (pp28–9).

In English the minutes come first – for example, ten to five; in Japanese the hour comes first – for example, **ichi ji** (*one o'clock*), **ni ji** (*two o'clock*), etc, followed by the minutes: **go fun** (*five minutes*), **jippun** (*ten minutes*). **Mae** is added for times before the hour: **ni ji jippun mae** (*ten to two* or literally *two o'clock ten minutes before*).

2 WORDS TO REMEMBER: TIME
4 minutes

Familiarize yourself with these words, then test yourself using the cover flap.

1時 **ichi ji**	one o'clock
1時5分 **ichi ji go fun**	five past one
1時15分 **ichi ji jyu-go fun**	quarter past one
1時20分 **ichi ji nijippun**	twenty past one
1時半 **ichi ji han**	half past one
1時45分 **ichi ji yonjyu-go fun**	quarter to two (literally *one forty-five*)
2時10分前 **ni ji jippun mae**	ten to two

3 USEFUL PHRASES
2 minutes

Learn these phrases, then test yourself using the cover flap.

今何時ですか?
ima nanji desuka
What time is it?

朝食は何時がいいですか?
chohshoku wa nanji ga iidesuka
At what time do you want breakfast?

12時に予約を入れています。
jyu-ni ji ni yoyaku o ireteimasu
I have a reservation for twelve o'clock.

4 WORDS TO REMEMBER: HIGHER NUMBERS

6 minutes

Japanese numbers are very logical. To count above ten, the individual numbers are simply spoken together. So 11 is **jyu-ichi** (*ten-one*), 15 is **jyu-go** (*ten-five*), etc. Be careful, though, to put the numbers the right way around: **go-jyu** is 50 (*five-ten*), **nana-jyu** is 70 (*seven-ten*). Units are added directly after the tens: 68 is **roku-jyu hachi**, 25 is **ni-jyu go**, and so on.

Pay special attention to the number 10,000, which is **man** or **ichi-man** (*one ten thousand*). A million is **hyaku-man** (*one hundred ten thousands*). Familiarize yourself with these words, then test yourself using the cover flap.

コンタクレス決済で八千円払いました。
kontakutoresu kessai de hassen en haraimashita
I've paid 8,000 yen by contactless payment.

eleven	十一	**jyu-ichi**
twelve	十二	**jyu-ni**
thirteen	十三	**jyu-san**
fourteen	十四	**jyu-shi/jyu-yon**
fifteen	十五	**jyu-go**
sixteen	十六	**jyu-roku**
seventeen	十七	**jyu-shichi**
eighteen	十八	**jyu-hachi**
nineteen	十九	**jyu-kyu**
twenty	二十	**ni-jyu**
thirty	三十	**san-jyu**
forty	四十	**yon-jyu**
fifty	五十	**go-jyu**
sixty	六十	**roku-jyu**
seventy	七十	**nana-jyu**
eighty	八十	**hachi-jyu**
ninety	九十	**kyu-jyu**
hundred	百	**hyaku**
three hundred	三百	**san-byaku**
thousand	千	**sen**
ten thousand	一万	**ichi-man**
two hundred thousand	二十万	**ni-jyu-man**
one million	百万	**hyaku-man**

5 SAY IT

2 minutes

twenty-five

sixty-eight

eighty-four

ninety-one

five to ten

half past eleven

What time is lunch?

Say the days of the week in Japanese (pp28–9).

Say **"three o'clock"** (pp30–31).

What's the Japanese for **"today"**, **"tomorrow"**, and **"yesterday"**? (pp28–9).

1 WARM UP
1 minute

Apo/(go)yoyaku
APPOINTMENTS

The tone of interactions is closely linked to the status of the people conversing. The formality of language used and the level of respect displayed towards a person depends on their social standing. A common way of establishing status is by the exchange of **meishi** (*business cards*). Business is conducted formally – use the honorific **san** to address senior colleagues unless invited to do otherwise.

2 USEFUL PHRASES
5 minutes

Learn these phrases, then test yourself using the cover flap.

おじぎ
ojigi
bow

明日お会いしましょうか? **ashita oai shimashohka**	Shall we meet tomorrow?
どなたとですか? **donata to desuka**	With whom? (formal)
いつお暇ですか? **itsu ohima desuka**	When are you free?
すみません。その日は忙しいです。 **sumimasen. sonohi wa isogashih desu**	Sorry. I'm busy that day.
木曜日はどうですか? **mokuyoh bi wa doh desuka**	How about Thursday?
大丈夫です。 **daijyohbu desu**	That's good for me.

ようこそ。
yohkoso
Welcome.

3 IN CONVERSATION

こんにちは。アポを入れているのですが。
konnichiwa. apo o ireteiru no desuga

Hello. I have an appointment.

だれとですか?
dare to desuka

With whom?

田中さんとです。
tanaka-san to desu

With Mr Tanaka.

4 PUT INTO PRACTICE

5 minutes

Complete this dialogue, then test yourself using the cover flap.

木曜日にお会いしましょうか？
mokuyoh bi ni oai shimashohka
Shall we meet on Thursday?

すみません。
その日は忙しいです。
sumimasen. sonohi wa isogashih desu

Say: Sorry, I'm busy that day.

いつお暇ですか？
itsu ohima desuka
When are you free?

火曜日の午後なら空いています。
kayoh bi no gogo nara aite imasu

Say: On Tuesday in the afternoon.

私も大丈夫です。
watashi mo daijyohbu desu
That's good for me, too.

何時がよろしいですか？
nanji ga yoroshih desuka

Ask: At what time?

4時はどうですか？
yoji wa doh desuka
At four o'clock, if that's good for you.

はい、大丈夫です。
hai, daijyohbu desu

Say: Yes, it's good for me.

---

4 minutes

そうですか。
何時のご予約ですか？
soh desuka. nanji no goyoyaku desuka

Very good. What time is the appointment?

3時です。
san ji desu

At three o'clock.

どうぞ、おかけください。
dohzo okake kudasai

Take a seat, please.

1 WARM UP

1 minute

Say "**I'm sorry**" (pp32–3).

What is the Japanese for "**I have an appointment**"? (pp32–3)?

How do you say "**With whom?**" in Japanese? (pp32–3).

Denwa de
ON THE TELEPHONE

The emergency number for the **shohboh-sha** (*fire service*) and **kyu-kyu-sha** (*ambulance*) is 119, while for the **kehsatsu** (*police*) it is 110, free from mobiles or fixed phones in Japan. To make international calls from Japan, dial the access code 010, country code, area code (omit the initial 0), and number. Japan's country code is 81. **Moshi moshi** (*hello*) is used to answer personal calls; business calls are more formal.

2 🔊 MATCH AND REPEAT

Match the numbered items to the list, then test yourself using the cover flap.

❶ イヤフォン
iyafon

❷ ヘッドフォン
heddofon

❸ 電話
denwa

❹ 携帯
kehtai

❺ チャージャー
chahjyah

❻ SIMカード
simu kahdo

❼ 留守番電話
rusuban denwa

❶ earphones

❷ headphones

❹ mobile phone

119

❺ charger

❻ SIM card

SIMカードをください。
simu kahdo o kudasai
I want to buy a SIM card, please.

3 🔊 IN CONVERSATION

お電話ありがとうございます。
ジャパニーズコネクションです。
odenwa arigatoh gozaimasu. japanihzu konekushon desu

Thank you for your call. This is Japanese Connection.

おはようございます。
岡田さんをお願いします。
ohayoh gozaimasu. okada-san o onegai shimasu

Good morning. (I'd like to speak to) Ms Okada, please.

どちら様ですか?
dochira sama desuka

May I know who's calling?

5 SAY IT
2 minutes

I'd like to speak to Mr Yamato.

Can I leave a message for Ms Kimura?

Can she call me back on Wednesday, please?

4 minutes

❸ telephone

answering machine ❼

4 🔊 USEFUL PHRASES
4 minutes

Learn these phrases, then test yourself using the cover flap.

ゴープレスプリンターの番号を教えてください。
gohpuresu purintah no bangoh o oshiete kudasai

I'd like the number for Gopress Printers.

岡田さんをお願いします。
okada-san o onegai shimasu

(I'd like to speak to) Mr/Ms Okada, please.

メッセージを伝えていただけますか？
messehji o tsutaete itadake masuka

Can I leave a message?

すみません、番号を間違えました。
sumimasen, bangoh o machigae mashita

Sorry, I have the wrong number.

4 minutes

ゴープレスプリンターの前田美樹郎と申します。
gohpuresu purintah no maeda mikiro to mohshimasu

Maeda Mikiro of Gopress Printers.

すみません。ただ今話し中です。
sumimasen. tadaima hanashichu desu

I'm sorry. The line is busy.

岡田さんの方から連絡いただけますか？
okada-san no hohkara renraku itadake masuka

Can Ms Okada call me back, please?

Fukushu to kurikaeshi
REVIEW AND REPEAT

Kotae *Answers*
(Cover with flap)

Telephones

❶ 携帯
  kehtai
❷ 電話
  denwa
❸ ヘッドフォン
  heddofon
❹ SIMカード
  simu kahdo
❺ 留守番電話
  rusuban denwa

---

1 TELEPHONES

Name these items in Japanese.

❷ telephone

headphones ❸

❶ mobile phone

❺ answering machine

When?

❶ See you tomorrow.
❷ I work on Saturday.
❸ My birthday is in May.
❹ I have a reservation for today.

---

2 WHEN?

2 minutes

What do these sentences mean?

❶ dewa mata ashita
❷ doyoh bi ni shigoto o shimasu
❸ watashi no tanjyoh bi wa go gatsu desu
❹ kyoh yoyaku ga arimasu

Time

❶ 1時
  ichi ji
❷ 1時5分
  ichi ji go fun
❸ 1時15分
  ichi ji jyu-go fun
❹ 1時20分
  ichi ji nijippun
❺ 1時半
  ichi ji han
❻ 2時10分前
  ni ji jippun mae

---

3 TIME

3 minutes

Say these times in Japanese.

❶ ❷ ❸ ❹ ❺ ❻

Kotae *Answers*
(Cover with flap)

3 minutes

4 SIM card

4 SUMS

4 minutes

Say the answers to these sums in Japanese.

1 10 + 6 = ?
2 14 + 25 = ?
3 66 – 13 = ?
4 40 + 38 = ?
5 90 + 9 = ?
6 20 – 3 = ?

Sums

1 十六
jyu-roku
2 三十九
san-jyu kyu
3 五十三
go-jyu san
4 七十八
nana-jyu hachi
5 九十九
kyu-jyu kyu
6 十七
jyu-shichi

5 TO WANT...

3 minutes

Fill in the blanks with the correct word.

1 Yamato-san o onegai _____ .
2 omochi o _____ shimasu.
3 koko ni sain o itadake _____ .
4 tetsudatte _____ masuka.
5 bihru o _____ shimasu.
6 san _____ yoh no tehburu o onegai shimasu.

To want

1 します
shimasu
2 お願い
onegai
3 ますか
masuka
4 いただけ
itadake
5 お願い
onegai
6 人
nin

Eki de
AT THE STATION

Japan is famous for its clean, fast, and reliable train services. The network covers the entire country – there are local **futsu** and **kaisoku** commuter trains; **kyuko** and **tokkyu** express trains; and **shinkansen**, high-speed intercity "bullet" trains. Senior citizens and children under 11 years can get discounts. Fines are handed out to those travelling without a ticket.

---

2 🔊 **WORDS TO REMEMBER**

3 minutes

Familiarize yourself with these words, then test yourself using the cover flap.

駅 **eki**	station
プラットホーム **purattohohmu**	platform
電車 **densha**	train
チケット **chiketto**	ticket
片道 **katamichi**	single
往復 **ohfuku**	return
一等／二等車 **ittoh/nitoh sha**	first/second class carriage
乗り換え **norikae**	change (trains)

サイン
sain
sign

改札口
kaisatsu guchi
ticket barrier

乗客
jyohkyaku
passenger

この駅は混んでいます。
kono eki wa konde imasu
This station is crowded.

---

3 🔊 **IN CONVERSATION**

京都行きを二枚おねがいします。
kyoto iki o nimai onegai shimasu

Two to Kyoto, please.

往復ですか？
ohfuku desuka

Is that return?

はい。席の予約が必要ですか？
hai. seki no yoyaku ga hitsuyo desuka

Yes. Do I need to make seat reservations?

4 USEFUL PHRASES

5 minutes

Learn these phrases, then test yourself using the cover flap.

大阪への電車は遅れています。
osaka eno densha wa okurete imasu
The train for Osaka is late.

How much is a ticket to Nagasaki?	長崎行きのチケットはいくらですか？ **nagasaki iki no chiketto wa ikura desuka**
Can I use a credit card?	クレジットカードが使えますか？ **kurejitto kahdo ga tsukae masuka**
Do I have to change trains?	乗り換えしなければいけませんか？ **norikae shinakereba ikemasenka**
Which platform does the train leave from?	電車は何番ホームから発車しますか？ **densha wa nanban hohmu kara hassha shimasuka**
What time does the train leave?	電車は何時に発車しますか？ **densha wa nanji ni hassha shimasuka**

Cultural tip Most large railway stations have ticket offices and automatic ticket machines that accept credit and debit cards, cash, and payments via mobile and digital wallets. You can also use the Suica card, a rechargeable smart card. Departure and arrival boards display information in katakana, kanji, and English.

5 SAY IT

2 minutes

This train is crowded.

How much is a ticket to Osaka?

Which platform does the train for Tokyo leave from?

4 minutes

いいえ。56,000円になります。
ihe. goman rokusen en ni narimasu

No. That's 56,000 yen.

クレジットカードが使えますか？
kurejitto kahdo ga tsukae masuka

Can I use a credit card?

もちろんです。電車は1番ホームから発車します。
mochiron desu. densha wa ichiban hohmu kara hassha shimasu

Certainly. The train leaves from platform one.

1 WARM UP

1 minute

How do you say "**train**" in Japanese? (pp38–9).

What does "**norikae shinakereba ikemasenka**" mean? (pp38–9).

Ask "**When are you free?**" (pp32–3).

Iku to noru
TO GO AND TO TAKE

Iku (*to go*) and **noru** (*to take*) are essential verbs in Japanese. Japanese verbs do not change according to the subject, but do have different endings for the tense (present/past) or mood (requesting/wanting, etc). Note that there is no future tense; instead, the present tense is used, often with a time indicator such as **ashita** (*tomorrow*). Note also that the verb usually comes at the end of a sentence.

2 🔊 IKU: TO GO

6 minutes

The verb **iku** can be used by itself or with an ending. The present tense uses **-masu**: **ikimasu** (*go, am/are/is going*); its negative uses **-masen**: **ikimasen** (*don't go, am not/aren't/isn't going*). The past tense uses **ikimashita** (*went*) or **ikimasen deshita** (*didn't go*). The "wanting" mood ends in **-tai**: **ikitai** (*want to go*). Practise the sample sentences, then test yourself using the cover flap.

バスで仕事に行きます。
basu de shigoto ni ikimasu

I go to work by bus. (present)

タクシーでは仕事に行きません。
takushih dewa shigoto ni ikimasen

I don't go to work by taxi. (present negative)

富士山に電車で行きました。
fujisan ni densha de ikimashita

I went to Mount Fuji by train. (past)

昨日は大阪に行きませんでした。
kinoh wa osaka ni ikimasen deshita

I didn't go to Osaka yesterday. (past negative)

明日バスで仕事に行きます。
ashita basu de shigoto ni ikimasu

I'll go to work by bus tomorrow. (future)

京都に行きたいです。
kyoto ni ikitai desu

I want to go to Kyoto. ("wanting" mood)

富士山に行きます。
fujisan ni ikimasu
I'm going to Mount Fuji.

Cultural tip Taxis in Japan are commonly black or white, although some may be yellow or green. There's usually a light at the bottom of the windscreen: green for occupied and red for available. The taxis are scrupulously clean – drivers even wear white gloves. Note that the rear passenger door on the left is remote-controlled by the driver, so be careful you don't get knocked over. You can usually hail taxis in the street. Fares are calculated by the meter, with the exception of certain fixed-rate routes. Tips are not usual.

3 **NORU**: TO TAKE

6 minutes

Like **iku**, **noru**'s present uses **norimasu** (*take, am/are/is taking*) or **norimasen** (*don't take, am not/aren't/isn't taking*). The past uses **norimashita** (*took*) or **norimasen deshita** (*didn't take*), and the "wanting" mood is **noritai** (*want to take*). Practise the sample sentences, then test yourself using the cover flap.

今日は自転車に乗ります。
kyoh wa jitensha ni norimasu
I'm taking my bicycle today.

I take the 8 o'clock bus in the morning. (present)	朝8時のバスに乗ります。 **asa hachi-ji no busu ni norimasu**
I don't take the metro at rush hour. (present negative)	ラッシュアワーには地下鉄に乗りません。 **rasshu awah niwa chikatetsu ni norimasen**
I took a taxi. (past)	タクシーに乗りました。 **takushih ni norimashita**
I didn't take a "bullet" train. (past negative)	新幹線に乗りませんでした。 **shinkansen ni norimasen deshita**
I'll take the metro tomorrow. (future)	明日地下鉄に乗ります。 **ashita chikatetsu ni norimasu**
I want to take a flight. ("wanting" mood)	飛行機に乗りたいです。 **hikohki ni noritai desu**

4 **PUT INTO PRACTICE**

2 minutes

Complete this dialogue, then test yourself using the cover flap.

どこに行かれるのですか？
doko ni ikareru no desuka
Where are you going?

Say: I'm going to the station.

駅に行きます。
eki ni ikimasu

地下鉄に乗りたいですか？
chikatetsu ni noritai desuka
Do you want to take the metro?

Say: No, I want to take the bus.

いいえ、バスに乗りたいです。
ihe, basu ni noritai desu

三十四番のバスですよ。
san-jyu yon ban no basu desuyo
That'll be bus number 34.

Say: Thank you very much.

どうもありがとうございます。
dohmo arigatoh gozaimasu

Takushih to basu to chikatetsu

TAXI, BUS, AND METRO

1 WARM UP
1 minute

Say "**I'm going to the station**" (pp40–41).

Say "**I want to take the shinkansen**" (pp40–41).

Say "**fruit**" and "**meat**" (pp22–3).

In cities, taxis can be hailed in the streets, but in smaller places you may need to book in advance (pp40–41). To use any form of public transport, you can either buy a ticket or use the Suica smart card (pp38–9). There are also mobile apps you can use instead of tickets or the Suica card.

2 WORDS TO REMEMBER
4 minutes

Familiarize yourself with these words, then test yourself using the cover flap.

バス **basu**	bus
バス停 **basu teh**	bus stop
タクシー **takushih**	taxi
タクシー乗り場 **takushih noriba**	taxi rank
地下鉄 **chikatetsu**	metro
地下鉄の駅 **chikatetsu no eki**	metro station
線 **sen**	line/route
運賃 **unchin**	fare

88番のバスはここに
停まりますか?
**hachijyu-hachi ban no basu
wa kokoni tomarimasuka**
Does the number 88 bus
stop here?

3 IN CONVERSATION: TAXI
2 minutes

秋葉原までお願い
します。
**akihabara ma-de
onegai shimasu**

To Akihabara, please.

わかりました。
wakarimashita

Very well.

ここで降ろしてください。
kokode oroshite kudasai

Can you drop me
here, please?

4 USEFUL PHRASES

4 minutes

Learn these phrases, then test yourself using the cover flap.

A taxi to Ginza, please.

銀座までのタクシーを
お願いします。
**ginza ma-de no takushih
o onegai shimasu**

Please wait for me.

ちょっと待ってください。
chotto matte kudasai

What time is the next
bus to the airport?

空港行きの次のバスは何
時ですか？
**ku-koh iki no tsugi no
basu wa nanji desuka**

How do you get
to Asakusa?

浅草にはどうやって行けば
いいですか？
**asakusa niwa dohyatte
ikeba iidesuka**

How long is the
journey?

どのくらいかかりますか。
**donokurai kakari
masuka**

Cultural tip Tokyo, Osaka, and other major cities have extensive, efficient public transport systems, including bus, metro, and local trains. Metro and train lines are called **sen** (for example, Asakusa-sen), while bus lines use **ban**. Fares vary depending on distance.

6 SAY IT

2 minutes

To the station, please.

A taxi to the airport, please.

How do you get to Akihabara?

5 IN CONVERSATION: BUS

2 minutes

博物館へ行きますか？
**hakubutsukan e
ikimasuka**

Do you go to
the museum?

はい。あまり遠くない
ですよ。
**hai. amari tohku
naidesuyo**

Yes. It's not very far.

どこでおりるか教えて
もらえますか？
**doko de oriruka oshiete
mora-e masuka**

Can you tell me when
to get off?

Dohro de
ON THE ROAD

1 **WARM UP** 1 minute

How do you say "**A coffee, please**"? (pp24–5).

Say "**my father**", "**my sister**", and "**my son**" (pp10–11).

Say "**I'm going to Ginza**" (pp40–41).

Japanese **kohsoku dohro** (*motorways*) are marked by green signs, while national highways and urban areas have blue signs. Road signs are often written only in Japanese, so learn the Japanese script for your destination if you're driving. Motorways are fast but some can be expensive, with toll booths along the way. Toll is charged by sections and can be paid by cash or rechargeable cards such as Suica (pp38–9).

---

2 🔊 **MATCH AND REPEAT**

Match the numbered items to the list, then test yourself using the cover flap.

❶ トランク
toranku

❷ フロントガラス
furonto garasu

❸ 充電器
jyuhdenki

❹ 充電スタンド
jyuhden sutando

❺ ドア
doa

❻ タイヤ
taiya

❼ ヘッドライト
heddo raito

❽ 充電ケーブル
jyuhden kehburu

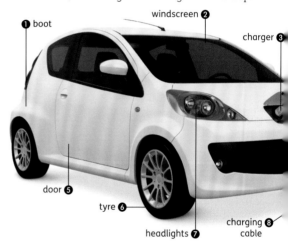

❶ boot
❷ windscreen
❸ charger
❺ door
❻ tyre
❼ headlights
❽ charging cable

Cultural tip Most petrol stations are manned but self-service is becoming popular. At self-service stations, the pump shows the fuel being added and the money owed. Electric cars can be charged at charging points and could take up to half a day to fully charge. You can pay for fuel by cash or card; you can also use apps for charging fees.

---

3 🔊 **ROAD SIGNS**

一方通行
ippoh tsu-koh
One way

徐行
jyokoh
Proceed slowly

最高速度
saikoh sokudo
Speed limit

4 🔊 USEFUL PHRASES

4 minutes

Learn these phrases, then test yourself using the cover flap.

The engine won't start.
エンジンがかかりません。
enjin ga kakari masen

Fill it up, please.
(literally *a full tank, please*)
満タンでお願いします。
mantan de onegai shimasu

4 minutes

charging ❹ point

5 🔊 WORDS TO REMEMBER

3 minutes

Familiarize yourself with these words, then test yourself using the cover flap.

car	車	**kuruma**
petrol	ガソリン	**gasorin**
diesel	ディーゼル	**dihzeru**
oil	オイル	**oiru**
engine	エンジン	**enjin**
gearbox	ギアボックス	**gia bokkusu**
flat tyre	パンク	**panku**
exhaust	エグゾースト	**eguzohsuto**
driving licence	運転免許証	**unten menkyosho**

6 SAY IT

1 minute

Diesel, please.

The car won't start.

I have a flat tyre.

2 minutes

止まれ
tomare
Stop

進入禁止
shin-nyu kinshi
No entry

駐車禁止
chu-sha kinshi
No parking

Fukushu to kurikaeshi
REVIEW AND REPEAT

Transport

❶ 車
kuruma

❷ 自転車
jitensha

❸ バス
basu

❹ タクシー
takushih

❺ 電車
densha

❻ 地下鉄
chikatetsu

1 TRANSPORT

Name these forms of transport in Japanese.

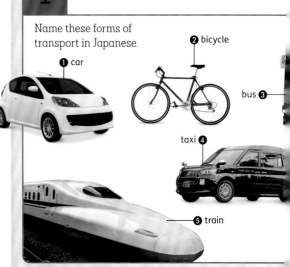

❶ car

❷ bicycle

bus ❸

taxi ❹

❺ train

Go and take

❶ 行きます
ikimasu

❷ 乗りたい
noritai

❸ 行く
iku

❹ 行かれる
ikareru

❺ 乗ります
norimasu

❻ 乗りました
norimashita

2 GO AND TAKE

4 minutes

Fill in the blanks with the correct form of
iku (*to go*) and **noru** (*to take*).

❶ **fujisan ni** _____ . (iku)

❷ **densha ni** _____ **desu.** (noru)

❸ **doko** _____ **no.** (iku)

❹ **doko ni** _____ **no desuka.** (iku)

❺ **ashita chikatetsu ni** _____ . (noru)

❻ **kinoh takushih ni** _____ . (noru)

3 minutes

6 metro

3 QUESTIONS

4 minutes

Ask these questions in Japanese.

❶ "Do you have any cakes?"

❷ "Do you have any children?"

❸ "What time is it?"

❹ "Do you go to the station?"

❺ "Where are you going?" (informal)

❻ "Can I use a credit card?"

4 TICKETS

4 minutes

You're buying tickets at a railway station. Join in the conversation, replying in Japanese following the numbered English prompts.

konnichiwa
❶ Two to Osaka, please.

ohfuku desuka
❷ No. Single, please.

niman hassen en ni narimasu
❸ What time does the train leave?

ni ji jippun mae desu
❹ Which platform does the train leave from?

purattohohmu wa ichiban desu
❺ Thank you very much.

Questions

❶ ケーキはありますか?
kehki wa arimasuka

❷ 子供さんはいますか?
kodomo san wa imasuka

❸ 今何時ですか?
ima nanji desuka

❹ 駅へ行きますか?
eki e ikimasuka

❺ どこ行くの?
doko iku no

❻ クレジットカード
が使えますか?
kurejitto kahdo ga tsukae masuka

Tickets

❶ 大阪行きを二枚お願いします。
osaka iki o nimai onegai shimasu

❷ いいえ。片道をお願いします。
ihe. katamichi o onegai shimasu

❸ 電車は何時に発車しますか?
densha wa nanji ni hassha shimasuka

❹ 電車はどのプラットホームから発車しますか?
densha wa dono purattohohmu kara hassha shimasuka

❺ どうもありがとうございます。
dohmo arigatoh gozaimasu

1 WARM UP
1 minute

Ask "**How do you get to the museum?**" (pp42–3).

Say "**I want to take the metro**" and "**I don't go by taxi**" (pp40–41).

Machi o mawaru
ABOUT TOWN

To talk about features or facilities, you can use the phrases **ga/wa arimasu** (*there is/are*) and **ga/wa arimasen** (*there isn't/aren't*). Note the word order is the opposite to English – for example, to say *there's a swimming pool near the bridge*, you would say **hashi no chikaku ni suimingu pu-ru ga arimasu** (literally *bridge/near to/swimming pool/there is*).

2 WORDS TO REMEMBER
4 minutes

Familiarize yourself with these words, then test yourself using the cover flap.

ガソリンスタンド **gasorin sutando**	petrol station
観光案内所 **kankoh an-naijyo**	tourist office
スイミングプール **suimingu pu-ru**	swimming pool
図書館 **toshokan**	library

3 MATCH AND REPEAT
4 minutes

Match the numbered locations to the list, then test yourself using the cover flap.

❶ 寺
tera

❷ 博物館
hakubutsukan

❸ 橋
hashi

❹ 美術館
bijutsukan

❺ デパート
depahto

❻ 噴水
funsui

❼ 広場
hiroba

❽ 駐車場
chusha jyo

❺ department store

fountain ❻

❶ temple

❷ museum

❸ bridge

❹ art gallery

4 🔊 USEFUL PHRASES

4 minutes

Learn these phrases, then test yourself using the cover flap.

Is there a museum in town?	街に博物館は ありますか？ **machi ni hakubutsukan wa arimasuka**
Is it far from here?	ここから遠い ですか？ **koko kara toh-i desuka**
There's a swimming pool near the bridge.	橋の近くにスイミング プールがあります。 **hashi no chikaku ni suimingu pu-ru ga arimasu**
There isn't a tourist office.	観光案内所はありません。 **kankoh an-naijyo wa arimasen**

五重塔は街の真ん中にあります。
gojyu no toh wa machi no mannaka ni arimasu
The five-storeyed pagoda is in the centre of town.

5 🔊 PUT INTO PRACTICE

2 minutes

Complete this dialogue, then test yourself using the cover flap.

お困りですか？
okomari desuka
Can I help you?

Ask: Is there an art gallery nearby?

近くに美術館はあります か？
chikaku ni bijutsukan wa arimasuka

いいえ、でも博物館はあ ります。
ihe, demo hakubutsukan wa arimasu
No, but there's a museum.

Ask: Is it far from here?

ここから遠いですか？
koko kara toh-i desuka

square ❼

駅の近くです。
eki no chikaku desu
It's near the station.

Say: Thank you.

ありがとうございます。
arigatoh gozaimasu

❽ car park

1 WARM UP
1 minute

How do you say "**Near the station**"? (pp48–9).

Ask "**Is there a museum in town?**" (pp48–9).

Ask "**Where are you going?**" (pp40–41).

Michi o kiku
ASKING FOR DIRECTIONS

Finding your way around an unfamiliar town or city can be confusing, so it's a good idea to learn how to ask for and understand directions. Remember that Japanese word order is different from English – for example, to say *turn left at the corner*, you would say **kado o hidari ni magette kudasai** (literally *corner at/left towards/turn/please*).

2 🔊 WORDS TO REMEMBER

Familiarize yourself with these words, then test yourself using the cover flap.

信号 **shingoh**	traffic lights
道路 **dohro**	road
道 **michi**	street
角 **kado**	corner
横断歩道 **ohdan hodoh**	crossing
地図 **chizu**	maps
オンライン地図 **onrain chizu**	online maps

ここはどこですか？
koko wa doko desuka
Where are we?

オフィスブロック
ofisu burokku
office block

公園
kohen
park

3 🔊 IN CONVERSATION

この街にレストランは
ありますか？
**kono machi ni resutoran
wa arimasuka**

Is there a restaurant
in town?

はい、駅の近くにあります。
**hai, eki no chikaku ni
arimasu**

Yes, near the station.

駅にはどうやって行けば
いいですか？
**eki niwa dohyatte
ikeba iidesuka**

How do I get to
the station?

5 SAY IT
2 minutes

Turn right at the traffic lights.

Turn left opposite the station.

It's about ten minutes by bus.

4 minutes

角を左に曲がってください。
kado o hidari ni magatte kudasai
Turn left at the corner.

4 USEFUL PHRASES
4 minutes

Learn these phrases, then test yourself using the cover flap.

(please) turn left/right	左／右に曲がってください **hidari/migi ni magatte kudasai**
on the left/ on the right	左に／右に **hidari ni/migi ni**
first street on the left	左側の最初の道 **hidari gawa no saisho no michi**
second street on the right	右の二番目の道 **migi no ni-banme no michi**
straight on	まっすぐに **massugu ni**
opposite	反対側 **hantai gawa**
at the end of the street	道の終わりに **michi no owari ni**
How do I get to the temple?	寺にはどうやって行けばいいですか？ **tera niwa dohyatte ikeba iidesuka**

道に迷いました。
michi ni mayoi mashita
I'm lost.

4 minutes

信号を左に曲がってください。
shingoh o hidari ni magatte kudasai

Turn left at the traffic lights.

遠いですか？
toh-i desuka

Is it far?

いいえ、5分くらいです。
ihe, go fun kurai desu

No, it's about five minutes.

1 WARM UP

1 minute

Say "**The third street on the left**" (pp50–51).

How do you say "**At six o'clock**"? (pp30–31).

Ask "**What time is it?**" (pp30–31).

Kankoh
SIGHTSEEING

Most major museums and art galleries close at least one day a week but are generally open on public holidays, while government buildings and private offices are closed on public holidays. Shops usually stay open until 10 or 11pm, but urban Japan is a 24/7 society and you will always find a few **konbini** (*convenience stores*) open at all times on all days.

2 WORDS TO REMEMBER

4 minutes

Familiarize yourself with these words, then test yourself using the cover flap.

ガイドブック **gaido bukku**	guidebook, travel guide
入場券 **nyu-jyo ken**	entrance ticket
割引／入場無料 **waribiki/ nyu-jyo muryoh**	discount/ free entrance
開館時間 **kaikan jikan**	opening times (museums, libraries)
営業時間 **eigyoh jikan**	opening times (shops, restaurants)
祝日 **shuku jitsu**	public holiday

ガイド付きツアー
gaido tsuki tsuah
guided tour

Cultural tip Japan has a range of visitor attractions, including some unusual ones like beer, sake, and fishcake museums; food factories; and electronics and cosmetics showrooms. Most charge entry fees, although some are free. Senior citizens, students, and people with disabilities may get free or reduced admission.

3 IN CONVERSATION

今日の午後は開いていますか?
kyoh no gogo wa aite imasuka

Do you open this afternoon?

はい、でも六時には閉まります。
hai, demo roku ji niwa shimari masu

Yes, but we close at six o'clock.

車いすは使えますか?
kurumaisu wa tsukae masuka

Is wheelchair access possible?

4 USEFUL PHRASES

3 minutes

Learn these phrases, then test yourself using the cover flap.

What time do you open/close?

何時に開きますか／閉まりますか。
nanji ni akimasuka/ shimarimasuka

Where are the toilets?

トイレはどこですか?
toire wa doko desuka

Is wheelchair access possible?

車いすは使えますか?
kurumaisu wa tsukae masuka

5 PUT INTO PRACTICE

4 minutes

Complete this dialogue, then test yourself using the cover flap.

すみません。博物館は閉館しました。
sumimasen. hakubutsukan wa heikan shimashita
Sorry. The museum is closed.

Ask: Do you open on Sundays?

日曜日はオープンしていますか?
nichiyo bi wa ohpun shite imasuka

はい、でも早く閉館します。
hai, demo hayaku heikan shimasu
Yes, but we close early.

Ask: At what time?

何時にですか?
nanji ni desuka

3 minutes

はい、あちらにエレベーターがあります。
hai, achira ni erebehtah ga arimasu

Yes, there's a lift over there.

ありがとう。チケットを四枚お願いします。
arigatoh. chiketto o yonmai onegai shimasu

Thank you. I'd like four tickets, please.

どうぞ。ガイドブックは無料です。
dohzo. gaido bukku wa muryoh desu

Here you are. The guidebook is free.

Ku-koh de
AT THE AIRPORT

Say in Japanese "**She is my aunt**" (pp14–15).

What's the Japanese for "**ticket**"? (pp38–9).

Say "**I'm going to Osaka**" (pp40–41).

Although the airport environment is largely international, it is sometimes useful to be able to ask your way around the terminal in Japanese. There are several international and domestic airports in Japan, with an extensive network of international, regional, and domestic flights operating out of them every day.

2 **WORDS TO REMEMBER**

4 minutes

チェックイン **chekku in**	check-in
出発 **shuppatsu**	departures
到着 **tohchaku**	arrivals
税関 **zeikan**	customs
入国審査／出国審査 **nyu-koku shinsa/ shukkoku shinsa**	passport control (entering/leaving Japan)
ターミナル **tahminaru**	terminal
搭乗口 **tohjyoh guchi**	boarding gate
便 **bin**	flight number

Familiarize yourself with these words, then test yourself using the cover flap.

23便は第2ターミナルから出発
します。
nijyusan-bin wa dai ni tahminaru kara shuppatsu shimasu
Flight 23 leaves from Terminal 2.

3 **USEFUL PHRASES**

3 minutes

Learn these phrases, then test yourself using the cover flap.

ロンドンからの飛行機は 予定通りですか？ **london kara no hikohki wa yotei dohri desuka**	Is the flight from London on time?
京都への飛行機は遅れて います。 **kyoto eno hikohki wa okurete imasu**	The flight to Kyoto is delayed.
荷物が見つかりません。 **nimotsu ga mitsukari masen**	I can't find my baggage.

4 PUT INTO PRACTICE

3 minutes

Complete this dialogue, then test yourself using the cover flap.

こんにちは、お待たせしました。
konnichiwa, omatase shimashita
Hello, thank you for waiting.
Ask: Is the flight to Osaka on time?

大阪への飛行機は予定通りですか?
osaka eno hikohki wa yotei dohri desuka

はい、予定通りです。
hai, yotei dohri desu
Yes, it's on time.
Ask: Which gate does it leave from?

どの搭乗口ですか?
dono tohjyoh guchi desuka

5 MATCH AND REPEAT

4 minutes

Match the numbered items to the list, then test yourself using the cover flap.

❶ check-in counter

passport ❷

ticket ❸

❹ boarding pass

❶ チェックインカウンター
chekku in kauntah

❷ パスポート
pasupohto

❸ チケット
chiketto

❹ 搭乗券
tohjyoh ken

❺ 機内持ち込み手荷物
kinai nochikomi tenimotsu

❻ カート
kahto

❼ スーツケース
su-tsu kehsu

hand ❺ luggage

trolley ❻

suitcase ❼

Fukushu to kurikaeshi
REVIEW AND REPEAT

Places

❶ 博物館
hakubutsukan

❷ 橋
hashi

❸ 美術館
bijutsukan

❹ 五重塔
gojyu no toh

❺ 寺
tera

❻ 広場
hiroba

1 PLACES

4 minutes

Name these locations in Japanese.

 ❶ museum

 ❷ bridge

 ❸ art gallery

 ❹ pagoda (five-storeyed)

 ❺ temple

 ❻ square

Car parts

❶ フロントガラス
furonto garasu

❷ 充電器
jyuhdenki

❸ 充電スタンド
jyuhden sutando

❹ ドア
doa

❺ タイヤ
taiya

❻ 充電ケーブル
jyuhden kehburu

2 CAR PARTS

Name these car parts in Japanese.

windscreen ❶

charger ❷

door ❹

tyre ❺

charging cable ❻

3 TRANSLATION

4 minutes

What do these sentences mean?

❶ hidari ni magatte kudasai

❷ kono machi ni hakubutsukan wa arimasuka

❸ mantan de onegai shimasu

❹ koko wa doko desuka

❺ hashi no chikaku ni suimingu puhru ga arimasu

❻ nanji ni akimasuka

❼ chiketto o yonmai onegai shimasu

Translation

❶ (Please) turn left.

❷ Is there a museum in town?

❸ Fill it up, please.

❹ Where are we?

❺ There's a swimming pool near the bridge.

❻ What time do you open?

❼ I'd like four tickets, please.

3 minutes

❸ charging point

4 DIRECTIONS

4 minutes

Ask how to get to these places in Japanese.

❶ temple

❷ railway station

❸ library

❹ petrol station

Directions

❶ 寺にはどうやって
行けばいいですか？

tera niwa dohyatte ikeba iidesuka

❷ 駅にはどうやって
行けばいいですか？

eki niwa dohyatte ikeba iidesuka

❸ 図書館にはどうやって
行けばいいですか？

toshokan niwa dohyatte ikeba iidesuka

❹ ガソリンスタンドにはどう
やって行けばいいですか？

gasorin sutando niwa dohyatte ikeba iidesuka

Heya no yoyaku
BOOKING A ROOM

WARM UP

1 minute

Ask in Japanese "**Can I use a credit card?**" (pp38–9).

Ask "**How much is that?**" (pp18–19).

Ask "**Do you have children?**" (pp12–13).

There are different types of accommodation in Japan: **hoteru** or standard international hotels; **ryokan**, traditional Japanese inns (pp62–3); **minshuku**, family-run B&Bs or guesthouses; and the famous tubular **kapuseruhoteru** (capsule hotels). **Rabuhoteru**, love hotels rentable by the hour, are best avoided. Airbnb, offering stays in private rooms and homes, is also popular.

---

2 **USEFUL PHRASES**

3 minutes

Learn these phrases, then test yourself using the cover flap.

朝食込みですか？
chohshoku komi desuka

Is breakfast included?

部屋からインターネットにアクセスできますか？
heya kara intahnetto ni akusesu dekimasuka

Does the room have internet access?

ルームサービスはありますか？
ru-mu sahbisu wa arimasuka

Is there room service?

チェックアウトは何時ですか？
chekkuauto wa nanji desuka

What time is check-out?

---

3 **IN CONVERSATION**

空いている部屋はありますか？
aiteiru heya wa arimasuka

Do you have any rooms?

はい、ダブルルームがございます。
hai, daburu ru-mu ga gozaimasu

Yes, we have a double room.

ルームサービスはありますか？
ru-mu sahbisu wa arimasuka

Is there room service?

4　WORDS TO REMEMBER

4 minutes

Familiarize yourself with these words, then test yourself using the cover flap.

部屋から海が見えますか？
heya kara umi ga mie masuka
Does the room have a sea view?

room	部屋	**heya**
single room	シングルルーム	**shinguru ru-mu**
double room	ダブルルーム	**daburu ru-mu**
twin room	ツインルーム	**tsuin ru-mu**
bathroom	バスルーム	**basu ru-mu**
shower	シャワー	**shawah**
balcony	バルコニー	**barukonih**
key	キー	**kih**
air-conditioning	エアコン	**eakon**
breakfast	朝食	**chohshoku**
two nights/ three nights	二泊／三泊	**ni haku/san paku**

5　SAY IT

2 minutes

Do you have any single rooms?

For two nights.

Is dinner included?

Cultural tip Japanese hotel rooms include a pair of house slippers (**surippa**) as a matter of course. It is assumed you will want to take off your shoes in the room, as you would at home. Hotel staff address customers using ultra-polite, uncommon Japanese expressions.

5 minutes

はい。何泊のご予定
ですか？
**hai. nan paku no
goyoteh desuka**

Yes. How many nights?

三泊です。
san paku desu

For three nights.

かしこまりました。
これがキーです。
**kashikomari mashita.
kore ga kih desu**

Very good. Here's your key.

1 WARM UP

1 minute

Ask "**Is there...?**" and reply "**There is...**" and "**There isn't...**" (pp48–9).

What does "**okomari desuka**" mean? (pp48–9).

Say "**I don't have any children**" (pp14–15).

Hoteru de
IN THE HOTEL

As well as slippers, you will nearly always find a traditional Japanese **yukata** (casual summer kimono/robe) in your room, usually laid out on the bed. This is the case even in the international chains. Non-smoking rooms are sometimes offered, but non-smoking floors are not always available. Bigger hotels and some guesthouses may include breakfast in the price of the room.

2 🔊 MATCH AND REPEAT

6 minutes

Match the numbered items to the list, then test yourself using the cover flap.

1 カーテン
kahten

2 クッション
kusshon

3 ソファ
sofah

4 ランプ
ranpu

5 枕
makura

6 ミニバー
minibah

7 ベッド
beddo

8 毛布
mohfu

9 ベッドスプレッド
beddo supureddo

10 ベッドサイドテーブル
beddo saido tehburu

1 curtains
2 cushion
3 sofa
4 lamp
5 pillow

8 blanket
9 bedspread

6 minibar
7 bed
bedside table **10**

Cultural tip Japanese bathrooms can sometimes be a culture shock to Western visitors. The bathtubs are smaller as they are only used for soaking yourself after you have cleaned off outside the tub. The toilets often feature high-tech gadgets, such as heated seats. Some even act as automatic bidets, with an in-built washer and drier.

3 USEFUL PHRASES

5 minutes

Learn these phrases, then test yourself using the cover flap.

The room is too hot/cold.　部屋が暑／寒すぎます。
**heya ga atsu/
samu sugi masu**

There aren't any towels.　タオルが ありません。
taoru ga arimasen

I'd like some soap.　石けんを下さい。
sekken o kudasai

The shower seems to
be broken.　シャワーが壊れて
いるようです。
**shawah ga kowarete
iruyoh desu**

The lift is not working.　エレベーターが壊れ
ています。
**erebehtah ga kowarete
imasu**

4 PUT INTO PRACTICE

3 minutes

Complete this dialogue, then test yourself using the cover flap.

はい、フロントでございます。　枕はありますか？
hai, furonto de gozaimasu　**makura wa arimasuka**
Yes, front desk.

Say: Are there any pillows?

部屋の担当者が
持って参ります。　それからテレビが壊れて
いるようです。
**heya no tantoh-sha ga
motte mairimasu**　**sorekara terebi ga
kowarete iruyoh desu**
The housekeeping staff
will bring you some.

Say: And the television
seems to be broken.

1 WARM UP
1 minute

Say "**hello**" (pp34–5).

What is the Japanese for "**the shower**" (pp60–61) and "**swimming pool**"? (pp48–9).

Say "**I'd like some towels**" (pp60–61).

Onsen to ryokan
HOT SPRINGS AND INNS

Onsen (*hot springs*) are an integral part of Japanese culture, deeply rooted in the country's history and traditions. Japan's vast array of onsen facilities include **sento**, affordable and accessible public bathhouses; **higeri-onsen**, day-trip hot springs; and **onsen-ryokan**, combining the charm of a **ryokan** with the therapeutic benefits of an **onsen**. Prices usually include accommodation and meals.

2 🔊 MATCH AND REPEAT

Match the numbered items to the list, then test yourself using the cover flap.

❶ ふすま
fusuma

❷ 座布団
zabuton

❸ ちゃぶ台
chabudai

❹ 浴衣
yukata

❺ 畳
tatami

❻ 掛け布団
kakebuton

❼ 布団
futon

❽ 敷き布団
shikibuton

screen door ❶

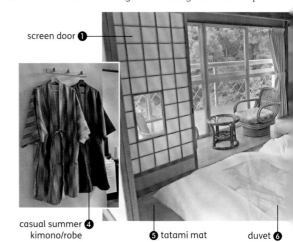

casual summer ❹ kimono/robe

❺ tatami mat

duvet ❻

3 🔊 IN CONVERSATION

二泊したいのですが。
ni haku shitai no desuga

I'd like to stay for two nights.

かしこまりました。
kashikomari mashita

Certainly.

この旅館に温泉はありますか?
kono ryokan ni onsen wa arimasuka

Is there a hot spring (tub) in the inn?

5 SAY IT
2 minutes

I'd like to stay for five nights.

Is there a swimming pool in the inn?

Can I rent a yukata?

How do I get to the higaeri-onsen?

4 minutes

or cushion **2** **3** low dining table

futon **7** **8** mattress

4 USEFUL PHRASES
3 minutes

Learn these phrases, then test yourself using the cover flap.

どんなタイプの温泉 ですか？
donna taipu no onsen desuka

What type of hot springs do you have?

サウナはありますか？
sauna wa arimasuka

Is there a sauna?

マッサージを予約 できますか？
massahji o yoyaku dekimasuka

Can I book a massage?

タオルを借りることが できますか？
taoru o karirukoto ga dekimasuka

Can I rent a towel?

5 minutes

はい、屋上にございます。
hai, okujoh ni gozaimasu

Yes, it's located on the roof.

タオルを借りることが できますか？
taoru o karirukoto ga dekimasuka

Can I rent a towel?

入り口で貸し出して おります。
iriguchi de kashidashite orimasu

You can rent one at the spa entrance.

1 **WARM UP**
1 minute

Say "**hot**" and "**cold**" (pp60–61).

What is the Japanese for "**room**" (pp58–9), "**bed**", and "**pillow**"? (pp60–61).

Setsumei
DESCRIPTIONS

Adjectives are words used to describe people, things, and places, and are quite simple to use in Japanese. For example, *car(s)* is **kuruma**, while *small car(s)* is **chihsai kuruma**. In a sentence, the word order is noun(s) + **ga/wa** (*as for*) + adjective + **desu** – for example, **kuruma wa chihsai desu** (*the car is small*) or **yama wa takai desu** (*the mountains are high*).

2 **WORDS TO REMEMBER**
7 minutes

There are no plurals in Japanese. So *the mountain is high* and *the mountains are high* would both be **yama wa takai desu**. Familiarize yourself with these words, then test yourself using the cover flap.

大きい **ohkih**	big, large
小さい **chihsai**	small
暑い／熱い **atsui/atsui**	hot (weather/material)
寒い／冷たい **samui/tsumetai**	cold (weather/material)
いい **ih**	good
悪い **warui**	bad
遅い **osoi**	slow
速い **hayai**	fast
うるさい **urusai**	noisy
静か **shizuka**	quiet
硬い **katai**	hard
柔らかい **yawarakai**	soft
美しい／綺麗 **utsukushih/kirei**	beautiful
醜い **minikui**	ugly
暗い **kurai**	dark
明るい **akarui**	light

寺は古いです。
tera wa furui desu
The temple is old.

森が綺麗です。
mori ga kireh desu
The forest is beautiful.

池 は大きいです。
ike wa ohkih desu
The pond is big.

橋は狭いです。
hashi wa semai desu
The bridge is narrow.

景色はとてものどかです。
keshiki wa totemo nodoka desu
The landscape is very peaceful.

3 USEFUL PHRASES

4 minutes

You can emphasize a description by using **totemo** (*very*) before the adjective or a form of **-sugiro** (*too*) at the end of the sentence. Learn these phrases, then test yourself using the cover flap.

The coffee is very hot.   コーヒーはとても熱いです。
koh-hi wa totemo atsui desu

My room is very noisy.   私の部屋はとても
うるさいです。
watashi no heya wa totemo urusai desu

This car is too small.   この車は小さすぎます。
kono kuruma wa chihsa sugimasu

This bed is very hard.   このベッドは硬すぎます。
kono beddo wa kata sugimasu

4 PUT INTO PRACTICE

3 minutes

Complete this dialogue, then test yourself using the cover flap.

こちらがお部屋です。   景色がとても 綺麗です。
kochira ga oheya desu   **keshiki ga totemo kirei desu**

Here's the room.

Say: The view is very beautiful.

バスルームはあちらです。   とても小さいです。
basu ru-mu wa achira desu   **totemo chihsai desu**

The bathroom is over there.

Say: It's very small.

あいにく他には部屋
はございません。   これにします。
ainiku hoka niwa heya wa gozaimasen   **kore ni shimasu**

Unfortunately, there aren't any other rooms.

Say: We'll take it.

Fukushu to kurikaeshi
REVIEW AND REPEAT

Kotae *Answers*
(Cover with flap)

Adjectives

❶ 大きい
ohkih

❷ 柔らかい
yawarakai

❸ 古い
furui

❹ 静か
shizuka

❺ 冷たい
tsumetai

---

1 ADJECTIVES

3 minutes

Fill in the blanks with the correct Japanese form of the adjective given in brackets.

❶ **ie wa** _____ **desu.** (big)

❷ **beddo wa** _____ **desu.** (soft)

❸ **tera wa totemo** _____ **desu.** (old)

❹ **watashi no heya wa** _____ **desu.** (quiet)

❺ **mizu ga totemo** _____ **desu.** (cold)

Inns

❶ ふすま
fusuma

❷ ちゃぶ台
chabudai

❸ 座布団
zabuton

❹ 浴衣
yukata

❺ 掛け布団
kakebuton

❻ 畳
tatami

❼ 布団
futon

---

2 INNS

Name these items in Japanese.

❶ screen door   low dining table

❹ casual summer kimono/robe   ❺ duvet   tatami ma

3 AT THE HOTEL

4 minutes

You are booking a room in a hotel. Join in the conversation, replying in Japanese following the numbered English prompts.

hai, dohzo
❶ Do you have any rooms?

hai. nanpaku no goyoteh desuka
❷ Five nights.

kashikomari mashita
❸ Is breakfast included?

ihe. go-hyaku en desu
❹ We'll take it.

kore ga kih desu
❺ Thank you very much.

Kotae *Answers*
(Cover with flap)

At the hotel

❶ 空いている部屋は
ありますか?
aiteiru heya wa arimasuka

❷ 五泊です。
go haku desu

❸ 朝食込みですか?
chohshoku komi desuka

❹ これにします。
kore ni shimasu

❺ ありがとうござ
います。
arigatoh gozaimasu

 floor cushion

3 minutes

4 NEGATIVES

5 minutes

Make these sentences negative using **wa arimasen**.

❶ taoru wa arimasu
❷ ru-mu sahbisu wa arimasu
❸ kono ryokan ni onsen wa arimasu
❹ kono machi ni hakubutsukan wa arimasu
❺ meishi wa arimasu

...uton

Negatives

❶ タオルはありません。
taoru wa arimasen

❷ ルームサービス
はありません。
ru-mu sahbisu wa arimasen

❸ この旅館に温泉は
ありません。
kono ryokan ni onsen wa arimasen

❹ この街に博物館は
ありません。
kono machi ni hakubutsukan wa arimasen

❺ 名刺はありません。
meishi wa arimasen

1 WARM UP
1 minute

Ask "**How do I get to the station?**" (pp50–51).

Say "**Turn left at the traffic lights**", "**Straight on**", and "**The station is near the the café**" (pp50–51).

Mise
SHOPS

Shopping malls (**shoppingu mohru**) have been on the rise in urban areas, typically housing shopping, dining, and entertainment options under one roof. Department stores (**depahto**) are popular, and many towns also have shopping arcades (**shotengei**), often set next to local train stations for convenience. You can also find independent shops in many towns.

2 🔊 MATCH AND REPEAT

The Japanese word **ya**, meaning *shop*, is added to words to indicate type or kind – for example, **pan ya** or baker (literally *bread shop*) and **niku ya** or butcher (literally *meat shop*). Match the numbered shops to the list, then test yourself using the cover flap.

❶ パン屋
   pan ya

❷ ケーキ屋
   kehki ya

❸ コンビニ
   konbini

❹ 肉屋
   niku ya

❺ デリカテッセン
   derikatessen

❻ 本屋
   hon ya

❼ 魚屋
   sakana ya

❽ 八百屋
   yao ya

❾ 豆腐屋
   tofu ya

❶ baker

❷ cake shop

❹ butcher

❺ delicatessen

❼ fishmonger

❽ greengrocer

Cultural tip Depahto often have a folk art section (**kyohdo zaiku**) selling traditional gifts such as painted wooden dolls, kimonos, fans, screens, lanterns, origami kits, and the famous Japanese **nurimono** (*lacquerware*). They also house specialized shops and may occasionally host exhibitions and local fairs. For everyday items, head to **konbini** (*convenience stores*), which sell newspapers, magazines, postage stamps, small groceries, snacks, **bento** (*boxed lunch*), and coffee.

花屋はどこですか？
hana ya wa doko desuka
Where is the florist?

3 USEFUL PHRASES

3 minutes

Learn these phrases, then test yourself using the cover flap.

Where's the hairdresser?	美容院はどこですか？ **biyoh in wa doko desuka**
Where can I pay?	どこで払えますか？ **doko de harae masuka**
I'm just looking. Thanks.	見ているだけです。どうも。 **mite iru dake desu. dohmo**
Do you sell SIM cards?	SIMカードを売っていますか？ **simu kahdo o utte imasuka**
I'd like to place an order for...	...を注文したいです。 **...o chu-mon shitai desu**
Can I exchange this?	交換できますか？ **kohkan dekimasuka**
Can you give me the receipt?	レシートをもらえますか？ **reshihto o morae masuka**

5 minutes

❸ convenience store

❻ bookshop

❾ tofu shop

4 WORDS TO REMEMBER

4 minutes

Familiarize yourself with these words, then test yourself using the cover flap.

antique shop	骨董品店 **kotto hin ten**
hairdresser	美容院 **biyoh in**
barber	床屋 **toko ya**
jewellery store	宝石店 **hohseki ten**
post office	郵便局 **yu-bin kyoku**
shoe shop	靴屋 **kutsu ya**
dry cleaner	ドライクリーニング屋 **dorai kurihningu ya**
pharmacy	薬局／薬屋 **yakkyoku/kusuriya**
souvenir shop	みやげ屋 **miyabe ya**

5 SAY IT

2 minutes

Where is the baker?

Do you sell fish?

I'd like to place an order for curtains.

1 WARM UP

1 minute

What is the Japanese for
"40", **"70"**, **"100"**, **"1,000"**,
and **"10,000"**? (pp30–31).

Say **"I'd like a big room"**
(pp64–5).

Ask **"Do you have a small
car?"** (pp64–5).

Denkiya de
AT THE ELECTRONICS STORE

Tokyo's Akihabara district, once known as "Electric
Town" for its many electronics and gadget shops,
has evolved over the years. While it continues to be
an electronics hub, it has also become a hotspot for
fans of manga, anime, video games, and aspects of
otaku culture. Home to themed cafés, hobby shops,
and arcades, it is a popular destination that offers
a unique blend of technology and pop culture.

2 🔊 MATCH AND REPEAT

Match the numbered items to the list,
then test yourself using the cover flap.

❶ ハードドライブ
hahdo doraibu

❷ 変換プラグ
henkan puragu

❸ マウス
mausu

❹ VR ヘッドセット
buiahru heddo setto

❺ USB フラッシュドライブ
USB furasshu doraibu

❻ ゲームコントローラー
gehmu kontorohrah

❼ ノートパソコン
nohto pasokon

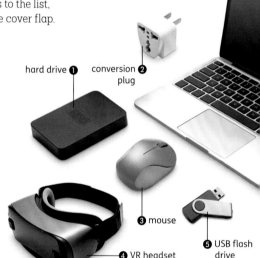

hard drive **❶**   conversion **❷**
plug

❸ mouse

❺ USB flash
drive

❹ VR headset

3 🔊 IN CONVERSATION

そのノートパソコン、いくら
ですか?
**sono nohto pasokon,
ikura desuka**

How much is that laptop?

税込み60万円です。
**zeikomi rokujyu-man
en desu**

It's 600,000 yen
including tax.

ハードディスクの容量はど
れくらいですか?
**hahdo disuku no yoryo
wa dorekurai desuka**

How big is the hard disk?

5 SAY IT

2 minutes

How much is the camera?

Do you have a laptop with 64 GB memory?

Where can I find the latest model?

4 minutes

⑦ laptop

⑥ game controller

4 ◀)) USEFUL PHRASES

5 minutes

Learn these phrases, then test yourself using the cover flap.

あのカメラは
高すぎます。
**ano kamera wa
takasugi masu**

That camera is too expensive.

あれはいくらですか？
a-re wa ikura desuka

How much is that one?

イギリスで使え
ますか？
**igirisu de tsukae
masuka**

Will it work in England?

Cultural tip The Japanese currency system is the *yen* (**en**, ¥). As each *yen* is worth less than 1p, you'll generally be spending thousands, or even tens of thousands of them. Banknote denominations go up to ¥10,000, so be careful not to confuse the number of zeros. Duty-free and tax-free shopping will give you the advantage of purchasing items at a lower cost and saving on various taxes.

3 minutes

8テラバイトで、メモリーは
96ギガバイトです。
**hachi terabaito de,
memori wa kyujyu-roku
gigabaito desu**

Eight terabytes, and it has 96 gigabytes of memory.

イギリスで使え
ますか？
**igirisu de tsukae
masuka**

Will it work in England?

はい、でも変換プラグが必
要です。
**hai, demo henkan
puragu ga hitsuyoh desu**

Yes, but you need a conversion plug.

1 WARM UP

1 minute

What are these items you could buy in a supermarket? (pp22–3).

yasai
kudamono
shihfu-do
kome
wain
mizu

Su-pah de
AT THE SUPERMARKET

Japanese supermarkets are often like hypermarkets, selling household items, clothes, food, and essentials. While cash is still accepted at most shops, cashless payment methods such as smart cards, digital wallets, and mobile payment apps have gained popularity. These alternative methods offer convenience, speed, and security, making them an appealing choice for shoppers and businesses.

2 🔊 MATCH AND REPEAT

5 minutes

Match the numbered items to the list, then test yourself using the cover flap.

❶ 化粧品
　keshoh hin

❷ 家庭用品
　kateh yoh hin

❸ 果物
　kudamono

❹ 飲み物
　nomimono

❺ 加工食品
　kakoh shokuhin

❻ 野菜
　yasai

❼ 冷凍食品
　reitoh shokuhin

❽ お菓子
　okashi

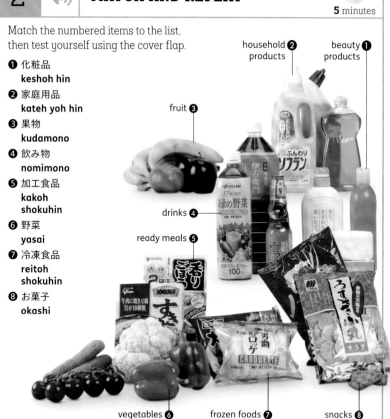

household products ❷
beauty products ❶
fruit ❸
drinks ❹
ready meals ❺
vegetables ❻
frozen foods ❼
snacks ❽

Cultural tip Following the COVID-19 pandemic, many shops and supermarkets adopted self-service check-outs, which made the process contactless and efficient. Supermarkets usually pre-package and price up fresh produce such as meat, fish, fruit, and cheese, making them easy to check out independently.

3 USEFUL PHRASES

3 minutes

Learn these phrases, then test yourself using the cover flap.

There is no need for a bag.	袋はいりません。 **fukuro wa irimasen**
Where is the drinks section?	飲み物類はどこですか? **nomimono rui wa doko desuka**
Where is the check-out?	レジはどこですか? **reji wa doko desuka**
Where are the shopping trolleys?	ショッピングカートはどこですか? **shoppingu kahto wa doko desuka**

4 WORDS TO REMEMBER

4 minutes

Familiarize yourself with these words, then test yourself using the cover flap.

milk	牛乳 **gyu-nyu**
bread	パン **pan**
butter	バター **batah**
ham	ハム **hamu**
salt	塩 **shio**
pepper	胡椒 **koshoh**
dairy products	乳製品 **nyu seihin**
washing powder	洗濯用洗剤 **sentaku yoh senzai**
washing-up liquid	食器用洗剤 **shokki yoh senzai**
toilet paper	トイレットペーパー **toiretto pehpah**
hand sanitizer	ハンドサニタイザー **hando sanitaizah**

5 SAY IT

2 minutes

Where is the dairy products section?

May I have some ham, please?

Where are the frozen foods?

1 WARM UP

1 minute

Say "**I'd like…**" (pp24–5).

Ask "**Do you have…?**" (pp14–15).

Say "**13**", "**24**", and "**30**" (pp30–31).

Say "**big**" and "**small**" (pp64–5).

Fuku to kutsu
CLOTHES AND SHOES

Loan words are used for most Western-style clothes: **shatsu** (*shirt*), **jyaketto** (*jacket*), etc. Only traditional clothing has Japanese names – for example, **kutsu** (*shoes*) and **sode** (*sleeves*). Other traditional articles, such as the **kimono**, **obi** (*sash*), and **geta** (*clogs*), are now largely reserved for special occasions. Note that clothes size is **fuku no saizu** and shoe size is **kutsu no saizu**.

2 ◀))) **MATCH AND REPEAT**

3 minutes

Match the numbered items to the list, then test yourself using the cover flap.

❶ シャツ
shatsu

❷ ネクタイ
nekutai

❸ ジャケット
jyaketto

❹ ポケット
poketto

❺ 袖
sode

❻ ズボン
zubon

❼ スカート
sukahto

❽ ストッキング
sutokkingu

❾ 靴
kutsu

shirt ❶
tie ❷
jacket ❸
pocket ❹
sleeve ❺
skirt ❼
trousers ❻
❽ tights
❾ shoes

Cultural tip Japan has its own system of sizes – even allowing for conversion of sizes, Japanese clothes tend to be cut smaller than English ones. For women's clothes, add one to get Japanese sizes. Measurements may vary according to brand, cut, and style, so it's best to try on clothes and shoes beforehand.

3 USEFUL PHRASES

5 minutes

Learn these phrases, then test yourself using the cover flap.

Would you please help me?	手伝っていただけますか？ **tetsudatte itadake masuka**
Do you have a larger size?	もっと大きいサイズがありますか？ **motto ohkih saizu ga arimasuka**
It's not what I want.	私の好みではありません。 **watashi no konomi dewa arimasen**
I'll take the pink one.	ピンクのを買います。 **pinku no o kaimasu**

4 WORDS TO REMEMBER

4 minutes

The character 色 **iro** (*colour*) is sometimes added to the basic words for colour listed here when they are used as nouns. Some colours become adjectives (pp64–5) by adding the characters い **i** or の **no** when describing an object – for example, 赤いシャツ **akai shatsu** (*red shirt*) and 緑のシャツ **midori no shatsu** (*green shirt*). Familiarize yourself with these words, then test yourself using the cover flap.

red	赤	**aka**
white	白	**shiro**
blue	青	**ao**
yellow	黄色	**ki iro**
green	緑	**midori**
black	黒	**kuro**

5 SAY IT

2 minutes

What shoe size?

I'll take the black one.

I'd like a 38.

Do you have a smaller size?

Fukushu to kurikaeshi
REVIEW AND REPEAT

Kotae *Answers*
(Cover with flap)

Electronic

❶ ゲームコントローラー
gehmu kontorohrah

❷ ハードドライブ
hahdo doraibu

❸ 変換プラグ
henkan puragu

❹ VRヘッドセット
buiahru heddo setto

❺ マウス
mausu

❻ USB フラッシュドライブ
USB furasshu doraibu

❼ ノートパソコン
nohto pasokon

1 ELECTRONIC
3 minutes

Name these electronic items in Japanese.

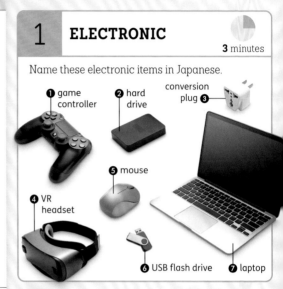

❶ game controller
❷ hard drive
conversion plug ❸
❺ mouse
❹ VR headset
❻ USB flash drive
❼ laptop

Description

❶ That camera is too expensive.

❷ My room is very noisy.

❸ Do you have a larger size?

2 DESCRIPTION
2 minutes

What do these sentences mean?

❶ ano kamera wa takasugi masu
❷ watashi no heya wa totemo urusai desu
❸ motto ohkih saizu ga arimasuka

Shops

❶ パン屋
pan ya

❷ 八百屋
yao ya

❸ 本屋
hon ya

❹ 魚屋
sakana ya

❺ ケーキ屋
kehki ya

❻ 肉屋
niku ya

3 SHOPS
3 minutes

Name these shops in Japanese.

❶ baker
❷ greengrocer
❸ bookshop
❹ fishmonger
❺ cake shop
❻ butcher

Kotae *Answers*
(Cover with flap)

4 SUPERMARKET

3 minutes

Name these products in Japanese.

❶ household products

❷ beauty products

❸ drinks

❹ snacks

❺ frozen foods

Supermarket

❶ 家庭用品
kateh yoh hin

❷ 化粧品
keshoh hin

❸ 飲み物
nomimono

❹ お菓子
okashi

❺ 冷凍食品
reitoh shokuhin

5 MUSEUM

4 minutes

You are buying entrance tickets at a museum. Join in the conversation, replying in Japanese following the numbered English prompts.

hai, dohzo
❶ I'd like four tickets.

sanzen nihyaku en ni narimasu
❷ That is very expensive!

waribiki wa arimasen
❸ How much is an audio guide?

nihyaku en desu
❹ Four tickets and four audio guides, please.

yonsen en ni narimasu
❺ Here you go. Where's the lift?

achira desu
❻ Thank you very much.

Museum

❶ チケットを4枚お願いします。
chiketto o yonmai onegai shimasu

❷ 高いですね!
takai desune

❸ オーディオガイドはいくらですか?
ohdio gaido wa ikura desuka

❹ チケット4枚とオーディオガイド4つ、お願いします。
chiketto yon-mai to ohdio gaido yottu, onegai shimasu

❺ これでお願いします。エレベーターはどこですか?
kore de onegai shimasu. erebehtah wa doko desuka

❻ ありがとうございます。
arigatoh gozaimasu

1 WARM UP

1 minute

Say "**Akiko is a student**" and "**I am a doctor**" (pp14–5), and ask "**Which platform?**" (pp38–9).

What is the Japanese for these family members: "**sister**", "**brother**", "**son**", "**daughter**", "**mother**", and "**father**"? (pp10–11).

Shigoto
JOBS

Japanese has some generic, non-job specific words used mainly to refer to office workers – for example, 会社員 **kaisha in** (*employee*). Office managers have different titles depending on their seniority: **shacho** (*MD*), **senmu** (*division*), **bucho** (*department*), **kacho** (*section*), and **kakaricho** (*team*). Most job titles in Japanese are gender neutral, with the same word applying to both the masculine and feminine forms.

2 🔊 WORDS TO REMEMBER: JOBS

7 minutes

Familiarize yourself with these words, then test yourself using the cover flap.

医者 **isha**	doctor
歯医者 **ha-isha**	dentist
看護師 **kangoshi**	nurse
先生 **sensei**	teacher
会計士 **kaikehshi**	accountant
弁護士 **bengo shi**	lawyer
デザイナー **dezainah**	designer
編集者 **henshuhsha**	editor
コンサルタント **consarutanto**	consultant
秘書 **hisho**	secretary
店主 **tenshu**	shopkeeper
電気技師 **denki gishi**	electrician
配管工 **haikankoh**	plumber
コック **kokku**	cook
エンジニア **enjinia**	engineer
自営業 **ji-eigyoh**	self-employed

会社を経営しています。
kaish o keiei shiteimasu
I run a company.

会計士です。
kaikehshi desu
I'm an accountant.

3 PUT INTO PRACTICE

4 minutes

Complete this dialogue, then test yourself using the cover flap. Note that when you state your occupation, you don't need the equivalent of a/an.

ご職業は？　会計士です。
goshokugyoh wa　**kaikehshi desu**
What's your profession?

Say: I'm an accountant.

どこの会社にお勤めですか？　自営業です。
doko no kaisha ni　**ji-eigyoh desu**
otsutome desuka
What company do you work for?

Say: I'm self-employed.

ああ、そうなんですか！　ご職業は？
ah, sohnan desuka　**goshokugyoh wa**
Oh, I see!

Ask: What's your profession?

編集者です。　妹も編集者です。
henshuhsha desu　**imohto mo**
I'm an editor.　**henshuhsha desu**

Say: My sister is an editor too.

4 WORDS TO REMEMBER:
WORKPLACE

3 minutes

Familiarize yourself with these words, then test yourself using the cover flap.

本社は大阪にあります。
honsha wa osaka ni arimasu
The head office is in Osaka.

head office	本社	**honsha**
branch	支店	**shiten**
department	部	**bu**
reception	受付	**uketsuke**
manager	マネージャー	**manehjyah**
office worker	会社員	**kaisha in**

Ofisu
THE OFFICE

An office environment or business situation has its own vocabulary in any language, but there are many items for which the terminology is virtually universal. Traditionally, most Japanese adults had an **inkan**, an official seal or stamp unique to them and used to sign papers and forms. You may still see these stamps on official papers and high-level contracts, although they are no longer a necessity.

1 WARM UP
1 minute

Practise different ways of introducing yourself in different situations (pp8–9). Mention your name, occupation, and any other information you'd like to give (pp8–9, pp14–15, pp78–9).

2 🔊 WORDS TO REMEMBER
5 minutes

Familiarize yourself with these words, then test yourself using the cover flap.

ミーティング **mihtingu**	meeting
コピー機 **kopihki**	photocopier ("copy machine")
コンピュータ **konpyu-tah**	computer
モニター **monitah**	monitor
マウス **mausu**	mouse
インターネット **intahnetto**	internet
メール **mehru**	email
パスワード **pasuwahdo**	password
ワイファイパスワード **wai fai pasuwahdo**	Wi-Fi password
コンファレンス **konfarensu**	conference
アジェンダ **ajenda**	agenda
手帳 **techoh**	diary
名刺 **meishi**	business card
ボイスメール **boisu mehru**	voicemail
印鑑 **inkan**	inkan (official seal)

3 🔊 MATCH

❶ wall clock

❹ telephone

❸ stapler   ❺ pen

notepad ❿   drawer ⓫

4 🔊 USEFUL PHRASES

2 minutes

Learn these phrases, then test yourself using the cover flap.

| I want to send an email. | メールを送りたいです。 **mehru o okuritai desu** |

| I need to make some photocopies. | コピーをとる必要が あります。 **kopih o toru hitsuyoh ga arimasu** |

5 SAY IT

2 minutes

I'd like to arrange a meeting.

Do you have a business card?

I have a laptop.

| I'd like to arrange an appointment. | アポを取りたいの ですが。 **apo o toritai no desuga** |

AND REPEAT

5 minutes

Match the numbered items to the list, then test yourself using the cover flap.

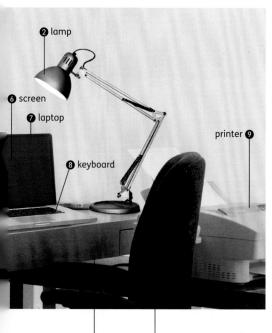

❷ lamp
❻ screen
❼ laptop
printer ❾
❽ keyboard
❷ desk
❸ swivel chair

❶ 時計 **tokei**
❷ ランプ **ranpu**
❸ ホチキス **hochikisu**
❹ 電話 **denwa**
❺ ペン **pen**
❻ 画面 **gamen**
❼ ノートパソコン **nohto pasokon**
❽ キーボード **kihbohdo**
❾ プリンター **purintah**
❿ ノート **nohto**
⓫ 引き出し **hikidashi**
⓬ 机 **tsukue**
⓭ 回転椅子 **kaiten isu**

1 WARM UP

1 minute

Say "**Oh, I see!**" (pp78–9), "**meeting**" (pp80–81), and "**appointment**" (pp32–3).

Ask "**What is your profession?**" and answer "**I'm an engineer**" (pp78–9).

Gakkai
ACADEMIC WORLD

In Japan, the first degree is **gakushi** (*bachelor's*), followed by **shuhshi** (*master's*) and then by **hakushi** (*PhD*). The bachelor's degree usually lasts four years. High schools often start to prepare for the competitive college entrance exams many years in advance as future prospects can depend on which university a student attends.

2 USEFUL PHRASES

3 minutes

Learn these phrases, then test yourself using the cover flap.

ご専門は？
gosenmon wa

What is your field?

生化学の研究をしています。
seikagaku no kenkyu o shite imasu

I am doing research in biochemistry.

法律を勉強しました。
hohritsu o benkyoh shimashita

I have a degree in law.

建築学の講師です。
kenchiku gaku no kohshi desu

I am a lecturer in architecture.

3 IN CONVERSATION

こんにちは。岡田です。
konnichiwa. okada desu

Hello, I'm Okada.

どこで教えていらっしゃいますか？
doko de oshiete irasshai masuka

Where do you teach?

東京大学です。
tokyo daigaku desu

I teach at Tokyo University.

4 WORDS TO REMEMBER

4 minutes

Familiarize yourself with these words, then test yourself using the cover flap.

見本市に出展しています。
mihonichi ni shutten shite imasu
We have a stand at the trade fair.

conference (academic)	学会	**gakkai**
trade fair	見本市／展示会	**mihonichi/tenjikai**
seminar	ゼミ	**zemi**
lecture	講義	**kohgi**
lecture theatre	講堂	**kohdoh**
exhibition	展示会	**tenjikai**
university lecturer	大学講師	**daigaku kohshi**
professor	教授	**kyohjyu**
medicine	医学	**igaku**
science	科学	**kagaku**
literature	文学	**bungaku**
engineering	工学	**kohgaku**
information technology	IT	**"ai-tih"**
law	法律	**hohritsu**
architecture	建築学	**kenchiku gaku**

5 SAY IT

2 minutes

I'm doing research in medicine.

I have a degree in literature.

She's a professor.

---

5 minutes

ご専門は？	物理です。研究もしています。	ああ、そうですか。
gosenmon wa	**butsuri desu. kenkyu mo shite imasu**	**ah, soh desuka**
What's your field?	Physics. I'm also doing research.	Oh, I see!

1 WARM UP

1 minute

Say "**I'm a businessman**" (pp78–9).

Say "**I want to send an email**" (pp80–81).

Say "**I'd like to arrange an appointment**" (pp80–81).

Bijinesu
IN BUSINESS

While on business trips to Japan, you will make a good impression and receive a more friendly reception if you make the effort to begin meetings with a short introduction in Japanese, even if your vocabulary is limited. After that, everyone will probably be happy to continue the meeting in English. Look out for the titles of managers (p78) when exchanging business cards.

2 WORDS TO REMEMBER

Familiarize yourself with these words, then test yourself by using the cover flap.

スケジュール **sukejyu-ru**	schedule
配達 **haitatsu**	delivery
支払い **shiharai**	payment
予算 **yosan**	budget
値段 **nedan**	price
書類 **shorui**	documents
請求書 **sehkyu-sho**	invoice
見積もり **mitsumori**	estimate
利益 **ri-eki**	profits
売り上げ **uri age**	sales
数字 **suhji**	figures
注文 **chu-mon**	order

契約書
kehyaku sho
contract

重役
jyu-yaku
executive

報告書
hohkoku sho
report

Cultural tip In general, business dealings are formal. However, the Japanese are famous for their hospitality. Visitors are often escorted from the start of the day until the end. It's a good idea to take presents from home to show your appreciation. It is common to exchange business cards when meeting someone for the first time – use both hands as it demonstrates respect for the person and acknowledges the importance of the professional relationship.

3 🔊 USEFUL PHRASES

6 minutes

Learn these phrases, then test yourself using the cover flap.

契約書を送っていただけ
ますか?
**kehyaku sho o okutte
itadake masuka**

Can you send me the
contract, please?

値段は決まりましたか?
**nedan wa
kimarimashitaka**

Have we agreed
a price?

配達はいつになりま
すか?
**haitatsu wa itsu ni
nari masuka**

When can you make
the delivery?

予算はおいくらですか?
**yosan wa oikura
desuka**

What's the
budget?

ここにサインをいただけ
ますか?
**koko ni sain o itadake
masuka**

Could I have your
signature here, please?

---

6 minutes

顧客
kokyaku
client

契約書を見せてください。
**kehyaku sho o misete
kudasai**
Please show me the contract.

4 SAY IT

2 minutes

Can you send me the
estimate, please?

Have we agreed
a price?

What are the profits?

Fukushu to kurikaeshi
REVIEW AND REPEAT

At the office

❶ 時計
tokei

❷ ノートパソコン
nohto pasokon

❸ ランプ
ranpu

❹ プリンター
purintah

❺ ホチキス
hochikisu

❻ ペン
pen

❼ ノート
nohto

❽ 机
tsukue

1 AT THE OFFICE

Name these items in Japanese.

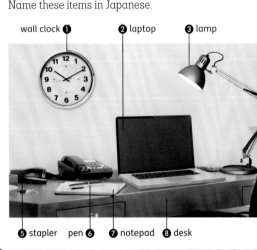

wall clock ❶   ❷ laptop   ❸ lamp

❺ stapler   pen ❻   ❼ notepad   ❽ desk

Jobs

❶ 医者
isha

❷ 配管工
haikankoh

❸ 店主
tenshu

❹ 会計士
kaikehshi

❺ 先生
sensei

❻ 弁護士
bengo shi

2 JOBS

3 minutes

Name these jobs in Japanese.

❶ doctor
❷ plumber
❸ shopkeeper
❹ accountant
❺ teacher
❻ lawyer

4 minutes

4 printer

3 WORK

4 minutes

Answer these questions following the numbered English prompts.

goshokugyoh wa
❶ Say "I'm a dentist".

doko no kaisha ni otsutome desuka
❷ Say "I'm self-employed".

doko de oshiete irasshai masuka
❸ Say "I teach at Tokyo University".

odenwa arigatoh gozaimasu
❹ Say "I'd like to arrange an appointment".

Work

❶ 歯医者です。
ha-isha desu

❷ 自営業です。
ji-eigyoh desu

❸ 東京大学です。
tokyo daigaku desu

❹ アポを取りたいの
ですが。
**apo o toritai no
desuga**

4 HOW MUCH?

4 minutes

Answer these questions in Japanese using the amounts given in brackets.

❶ koh-hi wa ikura desuka (¥600)

❷ heya wa ikura desuka (¥28,000)

❸ nohto pasokon wa ikura desuka (¥600,000)

❹ chiketto wa ikura desuka (¥20,000)

❺ kehki wa ikura desuka (¥800)

How much?

❶ 600円です。
roppyaku en desu

❷ 28,000円です。
**niman hassen
en desu**

❸ 600,000円です。
**rokujyu-man en
desu**

❹ 20,000円です。
niman en desu

❺ 800円です。
happyaku en desu

Karada
THE BODY

You are most likely to need to refer to the body in the context of illness or when speaking to a doctor. The most common phrases for talking about aches and pains are **...ga itai desu** (*I have a pain in my...*) and **...ga shimasu** (*I have...*) – for example, **zutsu ga shimasu** (*I have a headache*). Note that the ailment or body part comes first in the sentence.

2 ◀)) **MATCH AND REPEAT**: BODY
6 minutes

Match the numbered parts of the body to the list, then test yourself using the cover flap. Note that while spoken Japanese uses the same pronunciation for *leg* and *foot* (**ashi**), the written characters are different. There are also two separate words describing the back area: the *lower back* is **koshi**; the *upper back* is **senaka**.

❶ 髪
kami

❷ 頭
atama

❸ 首
kubi

❹ 肩
kata

❺ 腕
ude

❻ 胸
mune

❼ 肘
hiji

❽ お腹
onaka

❾ 膝
hiza

❿ 脚
ashi

⓫ 足
ashi

⓬ 手
te

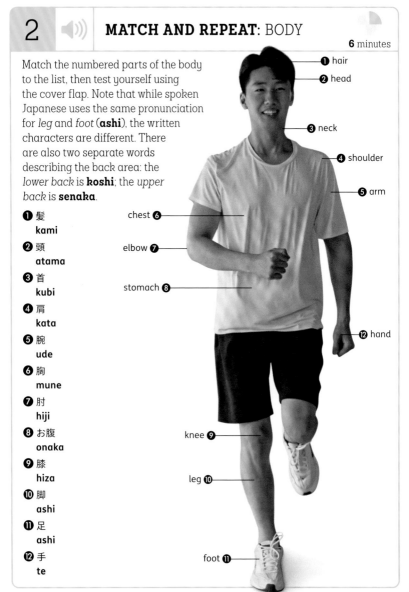

❶ hair
❷ head
❸ neck
❹ shoulder
❺ arm
chest ❻
elbow ❼
stomach ❽
⓬ hand
knee ❾
leg ❿
foot ⓫

3 MATCH AND REPEAT: FACE

3 minutes

Match the numbered facial features to the list, then test yourself using the cover flap. Note that Japanese doesn't have a separate plural, so **me** is both *eye* and *eyes*.

eye ❶

❷ eyebrow

❸ ear

❹ nose

❺ mouth

❶ 目 **me**

❷ 眉 **mayu**

❸ 耳 **mimi**

❹ 鼻 **hana**

❺ 口 **kuchi**

4 USEFUL PHRASES

3 minutes

Learn these phrases, then test yourself using the cover flap.

I have a pain in my lower back. 　腰が痛いです。 **koshi ga itai desu**

I have a rash on my arm. 　腕がかぶれています。 **ude ga kaburete imasu**

I don't feel well. 　調子が悪いです。 **chohshi ga warui desu**

5 PUT INTO PRACTICE

2 minutes

Complete this dialogue, then test yourself using the cover flap.

どうしましたか？ **doh shimashitaka** What's the matter? 　調子が悪いです。 **chohshi ga warui desu**

Say: I don't feel well.

どこが痛みますか？ **doko ga itami masuka** Where does it hurt? 　肩が痛いです。 **kata ga itai desu**

Say: I have a pain in my shoulder.

1 WARM UP

1 minute

Say "**I have a rash**" and "**I don't feel well**" (pp88–9).

Say the Japanese for "**red**", "**green**", "**black**", and "**yellow**" (pp74–5).

Yakkyoku de
AT THE CHEMIST

Japanese pharmacists study for at least six years before qualifying. They can give advice about minor health problems and are permitted to dispense both prescription and over-the-counter medicines. A chemist's or pharmacy is called **yakkyoku** or **kusuriya** and will usually have a large sign displaying the kanji for medicine 薬 (**kusuri**).

2 MATCH AND REPEAT

3 minutes

Match the numbered items to the list, then test yourself using the cover flap.

❶ 包帯
hohtai

❷ 目薬
megusuri

❸ シロップ
shiroppu

❹ 軟膏
nankoh

❺ 絆創膏
bansohkoh

❻ 注射器
chu-sha ki

❼ 座薬
zayaku

❽ 錠剤
jyohzai

bandage ❶

❷ eye drops

❸ syrup

❹ ointment

plaster ❺ syringe ❻ suppository ❼ tablet ❽

3 IN CONVERSATION

こんにちは。
どうしましたか？
konnichiwa. doh shimashitaka

Hello. What's the matter?

腹痛がします。
fukutsu ga shimasu

I have a stomach ache.

下痢気味ですか？
geri gimi desuka

Do you also have diarrhoea?

4 WORDS TO REMEMBER

2 minutes

Familiarize yourself with these words, then test yourself using the flap.

頭痛がします。
zutsu ga shimasu
I have a headache.

headache	頭痛	**zutsu**
stomach ache	腹痛	**fukutsu**
diarrhoea	下痢	**geri**
cold	風邪	**kaze**
cough	せき	**seki**
sunburn	日焼け	**hiyake**
toothache	歯痛	**ha-ita**

5 USEFUL PHRASES

4 minutes

Learn these phrases, then test yourself using the cover flap.

Do you have face masks? — マスクはありますか？ **masuku wa arimasuka**

Do you have that as a syrup? — それのシロップはありますか？ **sore no shiroppu wa arimasuka**

I'm allergic to penicillin. — ペニシリンにアレルギーがあります。 **penishirin ni arerugih ga arimasu**

6 SAY IT

2 minutes

I have a cold.

Do you have that as an ointment?

Do you have a cough?

3 minutes

いいえ、でも頭痛がします。
ihe, demo zutsu ga shimasu

No, but I have a headache.

これをお飲み下さい。
kore o onomi kudasai

Take this.

それの錠剤はありますか？
sore no jyohzai wa arimasuka

Do you have that as tablets?

Isha tono kaiwa
CONVERSATION WITH A DOCTOR

1 WARM UP
1 minute

Say "**I need some tablets**" and "**I need some ointment**"
(pp80–81 and pp90–91).

What is the Japanese for "**I don't have a son**"?
(pp14–15).

In an emergency, dial 119 for an ambulance. If it isn't urgent, book an appointment with a doctor and pay when you leave. You can usually reclaim the money if you have comprehensive travel and medical insurance. You may be able to find the names and addresses of local doctors at your hotel, the tourist office, or a pharmacy.

2 **USEFUL PHRASES YOU MAY HEAR**

3 minutes

Learn these phrases, then test yourself using the cover flap.

大したことはありません。 **taishitakoto wa arimasen**	It's not serious.
今飲んでいる薬はありますか? **ima nondeiru kusuri wa arimasuka**	Are you taking any medication?
骨折です。 **kossetsu desu**	You have a fracture.
入院が必要です。 **nyu-in ga hitsuyoh desu**	You need to stay in hospital. (literally *hospitalization is needed*)
口を開けてください。 **kuchi o akete kudasai**	Open your mouth.

検査が必要です。
kensa ga hitsuyoh desu
Tests are needed.

3 **IN CONVERSATION**

どうしましたか?
doh shimashitaka

What's the matter?

胸が痛いです。
mune ga itai desu

I have a pain in my chest.

診察しましょう。
shinsatsu shimashoh

I'll examine you.

4 USEFUL PHRASES YOU MAY NEED TO SAY

4 minutes

Learn these phrases, then test yourself using the cover flap.

妊娠しています。
ninshin shite imasu
I'm pregnant.

I'm diabetic.	糖尿病です。 **tohnyoh byoh desu**
I'm epileptic.	てんかん持ちです。 **tenkan mochi desu**
I'm asthmatic.	ぜんそく持ちです。 **zensoku mochi desu**
I have a heart condition.	心臓が弱いです。 **shinzoh ga yowai desu**
I feel breathless.	息が苦しいです。 **iki ga kurushih desu**
I have a fever.	熱があります。 **netsu ga arimasu**
It's urgent.	緊急です。 **kinkyu desu**
I'm here for my vaccination.	予防接種を受けに来ました。 **yoboh sesshu o ukeni kimashita**

Cultural tip Japan doesn't have a GP (general practitioner) system – people visit specialized clinics for minor symptoms and hospitals for serious issues. It's important to know which department/specialist you need. Many Japanese doctors speak good English, but you may need to briefly explain your problem in Japanese to a receptionist or nurse.

5 SAY IT

2 minutes

I have a pain in my arm.

My son needs to go to hospital.

Is it urgent?

5 minutes

重い病気ですか？
omoi byohki desuka

Is it serious?

いいえ、ただの消化不良です。
ihe, tadano shohka furyoh desu

No, you only have indigestion.

よかった！ 安心しました。
yokatta. anshin shimashita

Good! What a relief.

1 WARM UP

1 minute

Ask "**How long is the journey?**" (pp42–3).

Say "**Tests are needed**" (pp92–3).

What is the Japanese for "**mouth**" and "**head**"? (pp88–9).

Byoh-in de
AT THE HOSPITAL

Japanese medical care is excellent but very expensive, so make sure you have comprehensive insurance. General hospitals are called **sohgoh byoh-in**, while major teaching hospitals attached to universities are called **daigaku byoh-in**. It is useful to know a few basic phrases relating to hospitals for use in an emergency or in case you need to visit a friend or colleague in hospital.

2 USEFUL PHRASES

5 minutes

Learn these phrases, then test yourself using the cover flap.

訪問時間はいつですか？ **hohmon jikan wa itsu desuka**	What are the visiting hours?
ヒアリングループはありますか？ **hiaringu ru-pu wa arimasuka**	Is a hearing loop available?
どのくらいかかりますか？ **dono kurai kakari masuka**	How long does it take?
痛いですか？ **itai desuka**	Will it hurt?
ベッドに横になってください。 **beddo ni yoko ni natte kudasai**	Please lie down on the bed.
六時間何も食べないでください。 **roku jikan nanimo tabenaide kudasai**	Please do not eat anything for six hours.
頭を動かさないでください。 **atama o ugokasanai de kudasai**	Don't move your head.
血液検査が必要です。 **ketsueki kensa ga hitsuyoh desu**	A blood test is needed.
具合はいいですか？ **guai wa iidesuka** Are you feeling better?	

待合室はどこですか？
machiai shitsu wa doko desuka
Where's the waiting room?

看護師
kangoshi
nurse

医者
isha
doctor

3 WORDS TO REMEMBER

4 minutes

Familiarize yourself with these words, then test yourself using the cover flap.

emergency department	緊急病棟 **kinkyu byohtoh**
x-ray department	レントゲン室 **rentogen shitsu**
children's ward	小児病棟 **shohni byohtoh**
operating theatre	手術室 **shujyutsu shitsu**
waiting room	待合室 **machiai shitsu**
lift	エレベーター **erebehtah**
stairs	階段 **kaidan**

レントゲンは正常です。
rentogen wa seijyoh desu
The x-ray is normal.

4 PUT INTO PRACTICE

3 minutes

Complete this dialogue, then test yourself using the cover flap.

大したことはありません。
taishitakoto wa arimasen
It's not serious.

Ask: Are tests needed?

検査が必要ですか?
kensa ga hitsuyoh desuka

血液検査が必要です。
ketsueki kensa ga hitsuyoh desu
A blood test is needed.

Ask: Will it hurt?

痛いですか?
itai desuka

5 SAY IT

2 minutes

Is a blood test needed?

Where's the children's ward?

An x-ray is needed.

いいえ、大丈夫です。
ihe, daijyohbu desu
No, don't worry.

Ask: How long will it take?

どのくらいかかりますか?
donokurai kakarimasuka

Fukushu to kurikaeshi
REVIEW AND REPEAT

The body

❶ 頭
atama

❷ 腕
ude

❸ 胸
mune

❹ お腹
onaka

❺ 膝
hiza

❻ 脚
ashi

❼ 足
ashi

On the phone

❶ すみません、大和さんを
お願いします。
**sumimasen, yamato-
san o onegai shimasu**

❷ ゴープレスプリンター
の ジャック・ハントと
申します。
**gohpuresu purintah
no jack hunt to
mohshimasu**

❸ メッセージを 伝えて
いただけますか？
**messehji o tsutaete
itadake masuka**

❹ ミーティングは 火曜日
では ありません。
**mihtingu wa kayoh bi
dewa arimasen**

❹ ありがとう ございます。
arigatoh gozaimasu

1 THE BODY
4 minutes

Name these body
parts in Japanese.

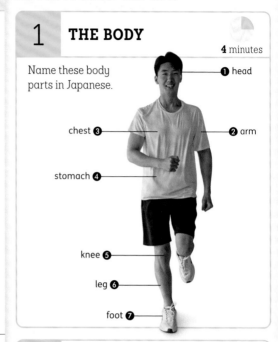

❶ head
chest ❸
❷ arm
stomach ❹
knee ❺
leg ❻
foot ❼

2 ON THE PHONE
4 minutes

You are arranging an appointment. Join in the
conversation, replying in Japanese following
the numbered English prompts.

**moshi moshi, japanihzu
konekushon desu**
❶ I'd like to speak to
Mr Yamato, please.

dochira sama desuka
❷ Jack Hunt of
Gopress Printers.

**sumimasenga, ima
hanashichu desu**
❸ Can I leave a message?

mochiron desu
❹ The meeting isn't
on Tuesday.

wakarimashita
❹ Thank you very much.

3 CLOTHING

3 minutes

Name these items of clothing in Japanese.

tie ❶

jacket ❷

❺ skirt

trousers ❸

❻ tights

shoes ❹

Clothing

❶ ネクタイ
nekutai

❷ ジャケット
jyaketto

❸ ズボン
zubon

❹ 靴
kutsu

❺ スカート
sukahto

❻ ストッキング
sutokkingu

4 AT THE DOCTOR'S

4 minutes

Say these sentences
in Japanese.

❶ I have a pain
in my leg.

❷ Is it serious?

❸ I have a heart
condition.

❹ Will it hurt?

❺ I'm pregnant.

At the doctor's

❶ 脚が痛いです。
ashi ga itai desu

❷ 重い病気ですか？
omoi byohki desuka

❸ 心臓が弱いです。
**shinzoh ga yowai
desu**

❹ 痛いですか？
itai desuka

❺ 妊娠しています。
ninshin shite imasu

1

WARM UP

1 minute

Say the months of the year in Japanese (pp28–9).

Ask "**Is there an art gallery?**" (pp48–9) and "**How much is that?**" (pp18–19).

Ie
AT HOME

In Japan, space is limited, and while you may see detached houses (**ikkenya**) in the suburbs or in more rural areas, most city dwellers live in blocks of flats (**apahto** or the more luxurious **manshon**). Rooms are often small and a combined kitchen and dining room (**dainingu kicchin**) is common. Earthquakes are frequent and buildings have to comply with strict specifications.

2 **MATCH AND REPEAT**

Match the numbered items to the list, then test yourself using the cover flap.

❶ 庇
hisashi

❷ 窓
mado

❸ 障子
shoji

❹ 壁
kabe

❺ 屋根
yane

❻ 階段
kaidan

❼ 雨どい
amadoi

❽ 縁側
engawa

❾ 引き戸
hikido

❿ 庭
niwa

eaves ❶   window ❷   ❸ paper window

steps ❻   gutter ❼   porch ❽   sliding door ❾

Cultural tip Most Japanese houses and multistorey buildings are built to withstand earthquakes and typhoons, using sturdy materials and structurally reinforced walls and windows. Most houses also have steel or wooden anti-typhoon shutters that can be closed quickly (buildings tend not to have shutters as there's a risk of secondary damage if they were to be blown away by strong winds). The typhoon season lasts from late August to early October, although storms can occur outside these months.

家賃は一月いくらですか?
**yachin wa hitotsuki
ikura desuka**
How much is the
monthly rent?

3 🔊 USEFUL PHRASES
3 minutes

Learn these phrases, then test yourself
using the cover flap.

車庫はありますか?
shako wa arimasuka

Is there a garage?

いつ入居できますか?
**itsu nyu-kyo
dekimasuka**

When can I move in?

家具付きですか?
kagu tsuki desuka

Is it furnished?

5 minutes

❹ wall ❺ roof

garden ❿

4 🔊 WORDS TO REMEMBER
4 minutes

Familiarize
yourself with
these words,
then test
yourself using
the cover flap.

room	部屋	**heya**
floor	床	**yuka**
ceiling	天井	**ten-jyoh**
attic	屋根裏	**yane ura**
bedroom	寝室	**shinshitsu**
bathroom	バスルーム	**basu ru-mu**
living room	居間	**ima**
dining room	ダイニングルーム	**dainingu ru-mu**
kitchen	台所	**daidokoro**
garage	車庫	**shako**

5 SAY IT
2 minutes

Is there a dining
room?

Where's the attic?

It's furnished.

Ie no naka de
INSIDE THE HOUSE

What's the Japanese for "**room**" (pp58–9), "**desk**" (pp80–81), "**bed**" (pp60–61), and "**window**"? (pp98–9).

How do you say "**This car is too small**"? (pp64–5).

When you rent a flat or house in Japan, the cost of utilities such as electricity and water may not be included in the rent, so be sure to check in advance with the homeowner or the **fudohsanya** (*estate agent*). You will be asked to pay a deposit called **shikikin**, which is refundable if the property is not damaged, as well as **reikin**, often the same amount as the deposit and considered a gift to the landlord.

2 ◀))) MATCH AND REPEAT

3 minutes

Match the numbered items to the list, then test yourself using the cover flap.

❶ 電子レンジ
denshi renji

❷ コンロ
konro

❸ 流し
nagashi

❹ 調理台
chohridai

❺ 炊飯器
suihanki

❻ 冷蔵庫
reizohko

❼ 戸棚
todana

❽ テーブル
tehburu

❾ 椅子
isu

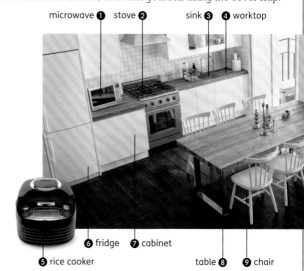

microwave ❶ stove ❷ sink ❸ ❹ worktop

❻ fridge ❼ cabinet

❺ rice cooker

table ❽ ❾ chair

3 ◀))) IN CONVERSATION

これが冷蔵庫です。
kore ga reizohko desu

This is the fridge.

炊飯器はありますか?
suihanki wa arimasuka

Is there a rice cooker?

はい、そしてこれが
コンロです。
hai, soshite kore ga konro desu

Yes, and here's the stove.

4 WORDS TO REMEMBER

2 minutes

Familiarize yourself with these words, then test yourself using the cover flap.

このソファは新しいです。
kono sofah wa atarashih desu
This sofa is new.

wardrobe	クローゼット	**curohzetto**
armchair	ひじかけ椅子／アームチェア	**hijikake isu/ahmu chea**
chest of drawers	たんす	**tansu**
carpet	絨毯	**jyu-tan**
bath	お風呂	**ofuro**
toilet	トイレ	**toire**
wash basin	洗面台	**senmendai**
tap	蛇口	**jyaguchi**
washing machine	洗濯機	**sentaku ki**

5 USEFUL PHRASES

4 minutes

Learn these phrases, then test yourself using the cover flap.

Are heat and electricity included?
光熱費込みですか？
kohnetsu hi komi desuka

I'm not fond of the curtains.
カーテンが気に入りません。
kahten ga kini irimasen

The fridge is broken.
冷蔵庫が壊れています。
reizohko ga kowarete imasu

6 SAY IT

2 minutes

Is there a washing machine?

The fridge is new.

The tap is broken.

---

3 minutes

流しが新しいですね？
nagashi ga atarashih desune

The sink is new, isn't it?

はい、それから食器洗い機もありますよ。
hai, sorekara shokki araiki mo arimasuyo

Yes. And there's even a dishwasher.

きれいなタイルですね！
kireh na tairu desune

What pretty tiles!

Niwa
THE GARDEN

Japanese gardens – often with water features, flowers like iris, hydrangea, and rhododendron, and trees like maple and cherry – can be seen in public places such as parks, temples, and hotels. Space constraints mean that many Japanese houses don't have their own gardens, but house plants, bonsai, and flower arrangements are popular. Blocks of flats may have communal gardens for residents.

---

1 WARM UP

1 minute

What's the Japanese for "**day**" and "**month**"? (pp28–9).

Say "**Where can I pay?**" (pp68–9) and "**Is there a garage?**" (pp98–9).

---

2 ◀))) WORDS TO REMEMBER

3 minutes

Familiarize yourself with these words, then test yourself using the cover flap.

春 **haru**	spring
夏 **natsu**	summer
秋 **aki**	autumn
冬 **fuyu**	winter
季節 **kisetsu**	season

---

3 ◀))) MATCH AND REPEAT

Match the numbered items to the list, then test yourself using the cover flap.

tree ❶

bushes ❷

path ❸

grass ❹

4 USEFUL PHRASES

4 minutes

Learn these phrases, then test yourself using the cover flap.

| I like the pond. | 池が好きです。
ike ga suki desu |

| What beautiful flowers! | きれいな花ですね！
kireh na hana desune |

| Can we walk in the garden? | 庭を歩いていいですか？
niwa o aruite ihdesuka |

| What kind of tree is this? | これは何の木ですか？
kore wa nanno ki desuka |

5 minutes

⑤ leaves

⑥ bridge

⑦ flowers

⑧ plants

⑨ rocks

⑩ pond

❶ 木	ki
❷ 低木	teiboku
❸ 小道	komichi
❹ 草	kusa
❺ 葉	ha
❻ 橋	hashi
❼ 花	hana
❽ 植物	shokubutsu
❾ 岩	iwa
❿ 池	ike

5 SAY IT

2 minutes

What kind of flower is this?

I like the waterfall.

Is there a pond?

Dohbutsu
ANIMALS

About 30 per cent of Japanese households include at least one pet, who is often treated like a member of the family. As there usually isn't enough space indoors for large animals, the most popular pets are small dogs, cats, and fish. Pet passports may be available to allow travellers to take their pets with them to Japan. Consult your vet for details of how to obtain the necessary vaccinations and paperwork.

1 WARM UP
1 minute

Say "**My name is John**" (pp8–9).

How do you say "**Don't worry**"? (pp94–5).

What is "**fish**" in Japanese? (pp22–3).

2 🔊 MATCH AND REPEAT

Match the numbered animals to the list, then test yourself using the cover flap.

❶ 猫
neko

❷ 魚
sakana

❸ 鳥
tori

❹ 犬
inu

❺ 兎
usagi

❻ 馬
uma

fish ❷

❶ cat

❹ dog

❺ rabbit

3 🔊 USEFUL PHRASES
4 minutes

Learn these phrases, then test yourself using the cover flap.

この犬はおとなしいですか？
kono inu wa otonashih desuka
Is this dog friendly?

盲導犬を同伴できますか？
mohdohken o dohan dekimasuka
Can I bring my guide dog?

猫は苦手です。
neko wa nigate desu
I'm not keen on cats.

この犬は噛み付きませんよ。
kono inu wa kamitsuki masenyo
This dog doesn't bite.

あなたの猫ですか？
anata no neko desuka
Is this your cat?

Cultural tip Some buildings keep large dogs as guard dogs. Japanese dog breeds, such as the Kishuken, Shibaken, and Ainuken, are known for their toughness and are often employed as "yard" dogs, although they are now popular as pets too. Look out for warning notices such as **mohken ni chu-i** (*beware of the dog*).

3 minutes

bird ❸

❻ horse

4 🔊 WORDS TO REMEMBER

4 minutes

Familiarize yourself with these words, then test yourself using the cover flap.

あれは何という魚
ですか？
**a-re wa nanto yu
sakana desuka**
What's that fish called?

monkey	猿	**saru**
sheep	羊	**hitsuji**
cow	牛	**ushi**
pig	豚	**buta**
mouse	ネズミ	**nezumi**
vet	獣医	**ju-i**
bowl	ボール	**bohru**
collar	首輪	**kubiwa**
lead	リード	**rihdo**

5 🔊 PUT INTO PRACTICE

3 minutes

Complete this dialogue, then test yourself using the cover flap.

あなたの犬ですか？
名前は何ですか？
**anata no inu desuka.
namae wa nandesuka**

Is this your dog?
What's his name?

Say: Yes. His name is Ichiroh.

はい。イチローと
いいます。
hai. ichiroh to ihmasu

犬は苦手です。
inu wa nigate desu

I'm not keen on dogs.

Say: Don't worry.
He's friendly.

大丈夫です。
おとなしいですよ。
**daijyohbu desu.
otonashih desuyo**

Kotae *Answers*
(Cover with flap)

Fukushu to kurikaeshi
REVIEW AND REPEAT

Colours

❶ 白
   shiro
❷ 黄色
   ki iro
❸ 緑
   midori
❹ 黒
   kuro
❺ 赤
   aka
❻ 青
   ao
❼ ピンク
   pinku

1 COLOURS

4 minutes

Name these colours in Japanese.

❶ white
❷ yellow
❸ green
❹ black
❺ red
❻ blue
❼ pink

Kitchen

❶ 電子レンジ
   denshi renji
❷ コンロ
   konro
❸ 調理台
   chohridai
❹ 流し
   nagashi
❺ 炊飯器
   suihanki
❻ 冷蔵庫
   reizohko
❼ 戸棚
   todana
❽ テーブル
   tehburu
❾ 椅子
   isu

2 KITCHEN

Name these items in Japanese.

microwave **❶**   stove **❷**   worktop **❸**   **❹** sink

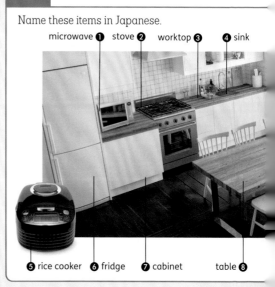

❺ rice cooker   **❻** fridge   **❼** cabinet   table **❽**

3 HOUSE

4 minutes

You are visiting a house in Japan. Join in the conversation, replying in Japanese following the numbered English prompts.

basu ru-mu wa kochira desu
❶ What pretty tiles!

daidokoro wa ohkih desu
❷ Is there a washing machine?

hai, sorekara shokki araiki mo arimasuyo
❸ Is there a garage?

ihe demo niwa ga arimasu
❹ Is it furnished?

mochiron desu
❺ How much is the monthly rent?

House

❶ きれいなタイル
ですね!
**kireh na tairu
desune**

❷ 洗濯機はありますか?
**sentaku ki wa
arimasuka**

❸ 車庫はありますか?
shako wa arimasuka

❹ 家具付きですか?
kagu tsuki desuka

❺ 家賃は一月いくらです
か?
**yachin wa hitotsuki
ikura desuka**

---

4 minutes

4 AT HOME

3 minutes

Name these things in Japanese.

❶ washing machine ❹ dining room
❷ sofa ❺ tree
❸ attic ❻ garden

❾ chair

At home

❶ 洗濯機
sentaku ki

❷ ソファ
sofah

❸ 屋根裏
yane ura

❹ ダイニングルーム
dainingu ru-mu

❺ 木
ki

❻ 庭
niwa

1 WARM UP

1 minute

Ask "**How do I get to the bank?**" and "**Where's the post office?**" (pp50–51 and pp68–9).

What's the Japanese for "**passport**"? (pp54–5).

Ask "**What time is the meeting?**" (pp32–3).

Ryohgaejo to ginkoh to yu-bin kyoku

BUREAU DE CHANGE, BANK, AND POST OFFICE

You can exchange currency at a bureau de change, major bank, or post office. You can also get cash at ATMs, but may be charged a fee. The post office also serves as a bank. Stamps are sold at the post office and at **konbini** (p68). Banks are usually open until 3pm and post offices until 4 or 5pm on weekdays.

2 ◀)) WORDS TO REMEMBER: POST

3 minutes

Familiarize yourself with these words, then test yourself using the cover flap.

ポスト **posuto**	postbox
小包 **kozutsumi**	parcel
手紙 **tegami**	letter
エアメール **ea mehru**	airmail
書留郵便 **kakitome yu-bin**	registered post
郵便配達人 **yu-bin haitatsu nin**	postman/ postwoman

イギリスへはいくらですか。
igirisu ewa ikura desuka
How much is it for the United Kingdom?

はがき **hagaki** postcard

切手 **kitte** stamps

封筒 **fu-toh** envelope

3 ◀)) IN CONVERSATION: BUREAU DE CHANGE

両替をお願いします。
ryohgae o onegai shimasu

I would like to change some money.

どのように両替しますか？
donoyohni ryohgae shimasuka

What would you like to exchange?

500ドルを円に両替してください。
gohyaku doru o en ni ryohgae shite kudasai

I would like to buy yen for five hundred dollars.

4 **WORDS TO REMEMBER**: BANK

2 minutes

Familiarize yourself with these words, then test yourself using the cover flap.

デビットカード
debitto kahdo
debit card

どんな支払い方法がありますか？
donna shiharai hohhoh ga arimasuka
What payment options are available?

bank	銀行 **ginkoh**
ATM/ cashpoint	ATM **"ATM"**
PIN	ピン、暗証番号 **pin, anshoh bangoh**
money	お金 **okane**
notes	紙幣 **shiheh**
coins	硬貨 **kohka**
credit card	クレジットカード **kurejitto kahdo**
contactless payment	コンタクレス決済 **kontakutoresu kessai**

5 **USEFUL PHRASES**

4 minutes

Learn these phrases, then test yourself using the cover flap.

I'd like to change some money.	両替をお願いします。 **ryohgae o onegai shimasu**
What is the exchange rate?	レートはいくら ですか？ **rehto wa ikura desuka**
What would you like to exchange?	どのように両替しますか？ **donoyohni ryohgae shimasuka**

6 **SAY IT**

2 minutes

I'd like a stamp for the United Kingdom, please.

Here's my credit card.

Where's the postbox?

3 minutes

かしこまりました。身分証明書はありますか？
kashikomarimashita. mibun shohmeisho wa arimasuka

Of course. Do you have any identification?

はい、これがパスポートです。
hai, kore ga pasupohto desu

Yes, here's my passport.

ありがとうございます。こちらが日本円になります。
arigatoh gozaimasu. kochira ga nihon en ni narimasu

Thank you, here are your yen.

1 WARM UP

1 minute

What is the Japanese for **"The fridge is broken"**? (pp100–101).

Say **"today"** and **"tomorrow"** in Japanese (pp28–9).

Shu-ri
REPAIRS

You can combine the Japanese words on these pages with the vocabulary you learned in week 10 to help you explain basic problems and cope with arranging most repairs. When organizing building work or a repair, it's a good idea to agree the price and method of payment in advance. Real estate agents can also help with problems.

2 WORDS TO REMEMBER:
SERVICES

4 minutes

Familiarize yourself with these words, then test yourself using the cover flap. Note that the terms for jobs in Japanese are usually gender neutral.

配管工 **haikankoh**	plumber
電気技師 **denki gishi**	electrician
機械技師 **kikai gishi**	mechanic
建築者 **kenchikusha**	builder
塗装工 **tosohkoh**	decorator
大工 **daiku**	carpenter
ブロック工 **burokkukoh**	bricklayer
清掃業者 **seisoh gyohsha**	cleaning staff
コンピューター修理工 **konpyu-tah shu-ri-koh**	computer repairperson

機械技師は必要ないです。
kikai gishi wa hitsuyoh nai desu
I don't need a mechanic.

3 IN CONVERSATION

おはようございます。
山田ですが。
**ohayoh gozaimasu.
yamada desuga**

Good morning.
This is Mrs Yamada.

おはようございます。
どうかなさいましたか?
**ohayoh gozaimasu.
dohka nasai mashitaka**

Good morning. Is there anything wrong?

食器洗い機が壊れて
います。
**shokki araiki ga
kowarete imasu**

The dishwasher is broken.

4 USEFUL PHRASES

3 minutes

Learn these phrases, then test yourself using the cover flap.

バスルームを掃除してください。
basu ru-mu o sohji shite kudasai
Please clean the bathroom.

Can you repair the television?	テレビを修理してもらえますか？ **terebi o shu-ri shite morae masuka**
Where can I get this repaired?	これはどこで修理してもらえますか？ **kore wa doko de shu-ri shite morae masuka**
Can you recommend a good repair shop?	良い修理屋を紹介してもらえますか？ **ih shu-ri ya o shohkai shite morae masuka**
It's possible to repair it today.	今日中に修理できるでしょう。 **kyohjyu-ni shu-ri dekiru deshoh**

5 PUT INTO PRACTICE

4 minutes

Complete this dialogue, then test yourself using the cover flap.

門が壊れています。
mon ga kawarete imasu
Your gate is broken.

Ask: Do you know a good carpenter?

いい大工さんを知っていますか？
ih daiku san o shitte imasuka

はい、村に一人います。
hai, mura ni hitori imasu
Yes, there is one in the village.

Say: Do you have the telephone number?

電話番号を知っていますか？
denwa bangoh o shitte imasuka

3 minutes

修理担当者を送ります。
shu-ri tantoh sha o okuri masu

We'll send a repairperson.

今日中に来てくれますか？
kyohjyu ni kite kure masuka

Can you do it today?

すみません。明日の朝になります。
sumimasen. ashita no asa ni narimasu

Sorry. But it will be tomorrow morning.

Kuru
TO COME

1 **WARM UP**
1 minute

Ask "**How do I get to the bridge?**" (pp48–9).

How do you say "**cleaning staff**"? (pp110–11).

Say "**It's 9:30**", "**10:45**", and "**12:00**" (pp30–31).

The verb **kuru** (*to come*) is another important verb. Like other verbs, it comes at the end of a sentence and does not change according to the subject. Remember there is no future tense and the present tense means both *I come* and *I'm coming*. As well as **kuru**, it is worth knowing the useful form **kite** (*come!*), which can be used with **kudasai** (*please*) for basic invitations.

2 **KURU**: TO COME

6 minutes

The verb **kuru** can be used by itself or with an ending. The present tense uses **kimasu** (*come, am/are/is coming*); its negative uses **kimasen** (*don't come, am not/aren't/isn't coming*). The past tense uses **kimashita** (*came*) or **kimasen deshita** (*didn't come*). The "wanting" mood ends in **-tai**: **kitai** (*want to come*). Note that **kuru** cannot be used when you are going somewhere – to say *I am coming (to you) now*, you would use *I am going (to you) now*. Practise the sample sentences, then test yourself using the cover flap.

庭師は毎週来ます。 **niwashi wa maishu kimasu**	The gardener comes every week. (present)
コックは日曜日には来ません。 **kokku wa nichiyohbi niwa kimasen**	The cook doesn't come on Sunday. (present negative)
大工さんは九時に来ました。 **daikusan wa kuji ni kimashita**	The carpenter came at nine o'clock. (past)
清掃業者は今日来ませんでした。 **seisoh gyosha wa kyoh kimasen deshita**	The cleaning staff didn't come today. (past negative)
明日車で来ます。 **ashita kuruma de kimasu**	I'm coming by car tomorrow. (future)
ここにまた来たいです。 **koko ni mata kitai desu**	I want to come here again. ("wanting" mood)

彼らは電車で来ます。
karera wa densha de kimasu
They're coming by train.

Conversational tip Beware of English phrases using *come* that translate differently in Japanese. For example, the Japanese equivalent of *I come from Australia* would be **ohsutoraria jin desu**, literally *Australia person I am*, or more commonly **ohsutoraria kara kimashita**, literally *came from Australia*.

3 USEFUL PHRASES

4 minutes

There are different expressions for invitations depending on the level of formality. Learn these phrases, then test yourself using the cover flap.

うちに午前10時に来てください。
uchi ni gozen ju-ji ni kite kudasai
Please come to my house at 10am.

Come over anytime! (informal, only friends and family)	いつでも遊びに来てね。 **itsudemo asobini kitene**
Please could you come to repair the pipe right away? (formal)	今すぐパイプを直しに来ていただけますか？ **imasugu paipu o naoshi ni kite itadake masuka**
Please could you come to the meeting tomorrow? (very formal)	明日会議にお越し願えますでしょうか？ **ashita kaigi ni okoshi negaemasu deshohka**

4 PUT INTO PRACTICE

4 minutes

Complete this dialogue, then test yourself using the cover flap.

明日午後1時着の電車で来ます。
ashita gogo ichi-ji chaku no densha de kimasu

I'll come by the train arriving at 1pm tomorrow.

Say: I will pick you up at the station.

駅に迎えに行きます。
eki ni mukae ni ikimasu

どこに行けばいいですか？
doko ni ikeba iidesuka

Where should I meet you?

Say: Please come to the north exit.

北口に来てください。
kita-guchi ni kite kudasai

分かりました。かばん一つで来ます。
wakarimasita. kaban hitotsu de kimasu

Okay. I'll be coming with one bag.

Say: No problem, see you tomorrow.

大丈夫です。では明日。
daijyohbu desu. dewa ashita

Kehsatsu to hanzai
POLICE AND CRIME

1 WARM UP
1 minute

What's the Japanese for **"big/large"** and **"small"**? (pp64–5).

Say **"The room is big"** and **"The bed is small"** (pp64–5).

If you are the victim of a crime while in Japan, you should go to a police station to report it. In an emergency you can dial 110. You may have to explain your complaint in Japanese, so some basic vocabulary is useful. In the event of a burglary, the police will usually come to the house.

2 **WORDS TO REMEMBER**: CRIME
4 minutes

Familiarize yourself with these words, then test yourself using the cover flap.

強盗 **gohtoh**	burglary
被害届け **higai-todoke**	police report
どろぼう **doroboh**	thief/burglar
警察官 **kehsatsu kan**	police officer
報告書 **hohkoku sho**	statement
証人 **shoh nin**	witness
目撃者 **mokugeki sha**	eyewitness
弁護士 **bengo shi**	lawyer

弁護士が必要です。
bengo shi ga hitsuyoh desu
I need a lawyer.

3 **USEFUL PHRASES**
3 minutes

Learn these phrases, then test yourself using the cover flap.

強盗にあいました。 **gohgoh ni aimashita**	I've been burgled.
何が盗まれましたか? **nani ga nusumare mashitaka**	What was stolen?
犯人を見ましたか? **hannin o mimashitaka**	Did you see who did it?
いつおこりましたか? **itsu okori mashitaka**	When did it happen?

カメラ
kamera
camera

財布
saifu
wallet

お金
okane
money

4

WORDS TO REMEMBER:
APPEARANCE

5 minutes

Familiarize yourself with these words, then test yourself using the cover flap. Note that the terms **otoko** (*man*) and **onna** (*woman*) are informal or casual descriptors. More polite equivalents would be **danseh** and **jyoseh**.

man/men	男 **otoko**
woman/ women	女 **onna**
tall	高い **takai**
short	低い **hikui**
young	若い **wakai**
old	年を取った **toshi o totta**
fat	太った **futotta**
thin	痩せた **yaseta**
long/ short hair	髪の長い／短い **kami no nagai/mijikai**
spectacles	眼鏡 **megane**
beard	あごひげ **ago hige**
moustache	口ひげ **kuchi hige**

男は白髪混じりで眼鏡をかけていました。
otoko wa shiraga majiri de megane o kakete imashita
The man had hair streaked with grey and wore glasses.

女は背が高く髪が長かったです。
onna wa se ga takaku kami ga nagakatta desu
The woman was tall and had long hair.

5

 ## PUT INTO PRACTICE

2 minutes

Complete this dialogue, then test yourself using the cover flap.

男はどんな格好でしたか？
otoko wa donna kakkoh deshitaka

Can you describe him?

Say: He was short and fat.

背が低く太っていました。
se ga hikuku futotte imashita

髪は？
kami wa

And the hair?

Say: He had grey hair and a beard.

白髪であごひげを生やしていました。
shiraga de ago hige o hayashite imashita

Cultural tip Day-to-day policing is carried out by the **todōfuken keisatsu** (Prefectural Police) under the oversight of the **keisatsu choh** (National Police Agency), the central coordinating body of Japan's police system. Tokyo has its own Metropolitan Police Department (**keishi choh**), with officers in navy blue.

Fukushu to kurikaeshi
REVIEW AND REPEAT

Kotae *Answers*
(Cover with flap)

To come

❶ 私はバスで来ます。
watashi wa basu de kimasu

❷ 電気技師は昨日来ました。
denki gishi wa kinoh kimashita

❸ 弁護士者は今日来ませんでした。
bengo shi wa kyoh kimasen deshita

❹ 清掃業者は木曜日には来ませんでした。
seisoh gyohsha wa mokuyoh bi niwa kimasen deshita

Bank and post

❶ はがき
hagaki

❷ 小包
kozutsumi

❸ 封筒
fu-toh

❹ 切手
kitte

❺ デビットカード
debitto kahdo

---

1 TO COME

3 minutes

Say these sentences in Japanese, using the correct form of **kuru** (*to come*).

❶ I'm coming by bus.
❷ The electrician came yesterday.
❸ The lawyer didn't come today.
❹ The cleaning staff didn't come on Thursday.

2 BANK AND POST

4 minutes

Name these items in Japanese.

postcard ❶

❷ parcel

❸ envelope

stamps ❹

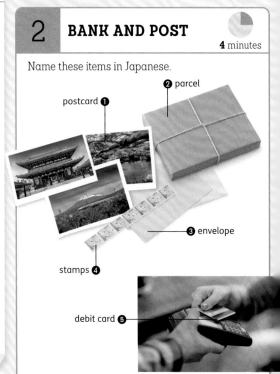

debit card ❺

3 APPEARANCE

4 minutes

What do these sentences mean?

❶ se ga hikuku yasete imashita

❷ otoko wa kami ga mijikakatta desu

❸ onna wa megane o kakete imashita

❹ otoko wa kuchi hige o hayashite imashita

❺ otoko wa shiraga de ago hige o hayashite imashita

Appearance

❶ He was short and thin.

❷ The man had short hair.

❸ The woman had glasses.

❹ The man had a moustache.

❺ He had grey hair and a beard.

4 THE PHARMACY

4 minutes

You are asking a pharmacist for advice.
Join in the conversation, replying in Japanese
following the numbered English prompts.

konnichiwa. doh shimashitaka
❶ I have a stomachache.

kaze gimi desuka
❷ No, but I have a headache.

kore o onomi kudasai
❸ Do you have that as a syrup?

hai, arimasu
❹ How much is that?

happyaku en ni narimasu
❺ Thank you very much.

The pharmacy

❶ 腹痛がします。
fukutsu ga shimasu

❷ いいえ、でも
頭痛がします。
**ihe, demo zutsu
ga shimasu**

❸ それのシロップは
ありますか？
**sore no shiroppu
wa arimasuka**

❹ いくらですか？
ikura desuka

❺ ありがとうござい
ます。
arigatoh gozaimasu

1 WARM UP

1 minute

What is the Japanese for "**museum**" and "**art gallery**"? (pp48–9).

Say "**I like the pond**" (pp102–3).

Ask "**What's your profession?**" (pp78–9).

Rejyah
LEISURE TIME

Japan offers many opportunities for cultural pursuits and modern leisure activities. The Japanese enjoy **shinrin-yoku** (*forest bathing*) and visiting **kankoh-chi** (*tourist spots*), and eating out and **tabe-aruki** (*walking food tours*) are also very popular. **Onsen** (pp62–3) are a great way to immerse yourself in Japanese culture. Be prepared for any of these topics to be the subject of conversation in social situations.

2 WORDS TO REMEMBER

Familiarize yourself with these words, then test yourself using the cover flap.

劇場	**gekijyoh**	theatre
音楽	**ongaku**	music
アート	**ahto**	art
映画	**eiga**	cinema/film
スポーツ	**supohtsu**	sport
旅行	**ryokoh**	travelling
ビデオゲーム **bideo gehmu**		video games
森林浴 **shinrin-yoku**		forest bathing

温泉が大好きです。
onsen ga daisuki desu
I love the onsen.

雪見温泉
yukimi onsen
snow-view onsen

湯けむり
yu kemuri
onsen mist

濁り湯
nigori yu
cloudy mineral-rich water

3 IN CONVERSATION

あきこさん、カラオケに行きませんか？
akiko-san, karaoke ni ikimasenka

Hi Akiko, do you want to go to a karaoke bar?

すみません、ちょっと用事があります。
sumimasen, chotto yohji ga arimasu

No thank you, I have other plans.

そうですか。残念です。
soh desuka. zannen desu

Well, that's a shame.

5 SAY IT
2 minutes

I'm interested in music.

I prefer sport.

I like the theatre.

I hate the cinema.

---

4 minutes

打たせ湯
utase yu
onsen waterfall

露天風呂
roten buro
open-air bath

---

4 🔊 USEFUL PHRASES
4 minutes

Learn these phrases, then test yourself using the cover flap.

What do you do in your free time? (formal/informal)	暇なときは何をしていますか／何してる？ **hima na toki wa nani o shite imasuka/nani shiteru**
What do you plan to do this morning? (formal/informal)	午前中、何をしますか／何するの？ **gozenchu, nani o shimasuka/nani suruno**
I prefer the cinema.	私は映画の方が好きです。 **watashi wa eiga no hohga sukidesu**
I'm interested in art.	アートに興味があります。 **ahto ni kyohmi ga arimasu**
I hate opera.	私はオペラは大嫌いです。 **watashi wa opera wa daikirai desu**
My hobby is reading.	趣味は読書です。 **shumi wa dokusho desu**

ビデオゲームが好きです。
bideo gehmu ga suki desu
I like video games.

---

4 minutes

温泉に行くんです。一緒に行きませんか。
onsen ni ikundesu. issho ni ikimasenka

I'm going to the onsen. Do you want to join me?

いいですね。でも、今日はカラオケに行きます。
ih desune. demo, kyoh wa karaoke ni ikimasu

That sounds nice, but I want to do karaoke today.

そうですか。じゃ、また今度！
soh desuka. jya, mata kondo

No problem. Next time!

Ask "**Do you want to go to a karaoke bar?**" (pp118–19).

Say "**I like the theatre**", "**I prefer music**", and "**I'm interested in reading**" (pp118–19).

Supohtsu to shumi
SPORT AND HOBBIES

Many Japanese people golf, ski, jog, and cycle, and spectator sports such as baseball, football, sumo, karate, and judo are very popular. The verb **shimasu** (*to do or to make*) is useful for talking about sports and hobbies. When talking about music, **hikimasu** (*to play*) is used for string instruments, **fukimasu** (*to blow*) for wind, and **tatakimasu** (*to hit*) for percussion.

2 🔊 **WORDS TO REMEMBER**

5 minutes

Familiarize yourself with these words, then test yourself using the cover flap.

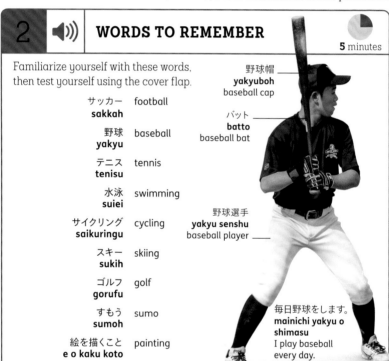

サッカー **sakkah**	football
野球 **yakyu**	baseball
テニス **tenisu**	tennis
水泳 **suiei**	swimming
サイクリング **saikuringu**	cycling
スキー **sukih**	skiing
ゴルフ **gorufu**	golf
すもう **sumoh**	sumo
絵を描くこと **e o kaku koto**	painting

野球帽
yakyuboh
baseball cap

バット
batto
baseball bat

野球選手
yakyu senshu
baseball player

毎日野球をします。
mainichi yakyu o shimasu
I play baseball every day.

3 🔊 **USEFUL PHRASES**

2 minutes

Learn these phrases, then test yourself using the cover flap.

毎日ゴルフをします。
mainichi gorufu o shimasu
I play golf every day.

彼はテニスをします。
kare wa tenisu o shimasu
He plays tennis.

彼女は書道が好きです。
kanojo wa shodo ga suki desu
She likes calligraphy.

4 PHRASES TO REMEMBER

4 minutes

Familiarize yourself with these phrases, then test yourself using the cover flap.

What do you like doing? (formal/informal)	何をするのがお好きですか／好き？ **nani o surunoga osuki desuka/suki**
I like playing golf.	ゴルフをするのが好きです。 **gorufu o surunoga suki desu**
I like going fishing.	魚釣りが好きです。 **sakana tsuri ga suki desu**
I go mountain climbing.	登山に行きます。 **tozan ni ikimasu**
I play tennis.	テニスをします。 **tenisu o shimasu**
I play the violin.	バイオリンを弾きます。 **baiorin o hikimasu**
I play the sax.	サックスを吹きます。 **sakkusu o fukimasu**
I play the drums.	ドラムを叩きます。 **doramu o tatakimasu**

今日はハイキング日和です。
kyoh wa haikingu biyori desu
It's nice weather for hiking today.

5 PUT INTO PRACTICE

3 minutes

Complete this dialogue, then test yourself using the cover flap.

何をするのがお好きですか？
nani o surunoga osuki desuka
What do you like doing?

サッカーをするのが好きです。
sakkah o surunoga suki desu

Say: I like playing football.

野球もなさいますか？
yakyu mo nasai masuka
Do you play baseball as well?

いいえ、ゴルフをします。
ihe, gorufu o shimasu

Say: No, I play golf.

Cultural tip With a history spanning centuries, the ancient sport of sumo wrestling (すもう **sumoh**) is considered Japan's national sport. Every year there are six 15-day tournaments held in Tokyo, Osaka, Nagoya, and Fukuoka, with three of these taking place in Tokyo. Tickets to watch the matches can be purchased online. Prices usually start from under 4,000 yen and vary according to the venue.

Shakohteki na bamen de
SOCIALIZING

1 **WARM UP**

1 minute

Say "**your husband**" and "**your wife**" (pp12–13).

How do you say "**lunch**" and "**dinner**" in Japanese? (pp20–21).

Say "**Sorry, I'm busy that day**" (pp32–3).

As a business guest, it's common to be invited to a restaurant. This is partly practical – people often have long commutes back to their home or hotel. But if you're staying for longer, you may be invited to someone's home for a meal or a party. It is polite to use あなた **anata** (*you*) when you don't know someone's name.

---

2 **USEFUL PHRASES**

Learn these phrases, then test yourself using the cover flap.

ディナーにいらっしゃいませんか？
dinah ni irasshai masenka
Would you like to come for dinner?

水曜日はいかが ですか？
suiyoh bi wa ikaga desuka
What about Wednesday?

また今度誘ってください。
mata kondo sasotte kudasai
Perhaps another time.

電話番号を教えていただけますか？
denwa bangoh o oshiete itadake masuka
Could I have your number, please?

招待者
shohtai sha
hostess

ご招待ありがとう ございます。
goshohtai arigatoh gozaimasu
Thank you very much for inviting us.

---

3 **IN CONVERSATION**

火曜日にディナーに
いらっしゃいませんか？
kayoh bi ni dinah ni irasshai masenka

Would you like to come for dinner on Tuesday?

すみません。火曜日は忙しいです。
sumimasen. kayoh bi wa isogashih desu

Sorry. I'm busy on Tuesday.

木曜日はいかがですか？
mokuyoh bi wa ikaga desuka

What about Thursday?

Cultural tip When visiting a Japanese home, remember to take off your shoes at the door. Carry a gift for the host – flowers, a bottle of drink, or a present from your home country will be appreciated.

4 🔊 WORDS TO REMEMBER

3 minutes

Familiarize yourself with these words, then test yourself using the cover flap.

party	パーティー	**pahtih**
dinner party	ディナーパーティー	**dinah pahtih**
reception	歓迎会	**kangeikai**
invitation	招待	**shohtai**
gift	お土産	**omiyage**

3 minutes

お客
okyaku
guest

5 🔊 PUT INTO PRACTICE

5 minutes

Complete this dialogue, then test yourself using the cover flap.

土曜日にパーティーを開く
のですが、お暇ですか?
**doyoh bi ni pahtih o hiraku
no desuga, ohima desuka**
We are having a party on
Saturday. Are you free?

Say: Yes, how nice!

はい、楽しみです!
hai, tanoshimi desu

ああよかった!
ah yokatta
That's great!

Say: At what time
should we arrive?

何時に伺いましょうか?
**nanji ni ukagai
mashohka**

3 minutes

はい、楽しみです!
hai, tanoshimi desu
Yes, how nice!

ご主人もご一緒に。
goshujin mo goissho ni
Bring your husband.

ありがとう。何時に
伺いましょうか?
**arigatoh. nanji ni ukagai
mashohka**
Thank you. At what time
should we arrive?

Kotae *Answers*
(Cover with flap)

Fukushu to kurikaeshi
REVIEW AND REPEAT

Animals

❶ 猫
  neko
❷ 鳥
  tori
❸ 魚
  sakana
❹ 兎
  usagi
❺ 馬
  uma
❻ 犬
  inu

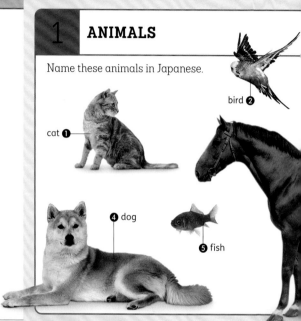

1 ANIMALS

Name these animals in Japanese.

bird ❷

cat ❶

❹ dog

❺ fish

I like…

❶ テニスをするのが好きです。
  tenisu o surunoga suki desu
❷ サッカーが好きではありません。
  sakkah ga suki dewa arimasen
❸ 野球をします。
  yakyu o shimasu
❹ 私は書道が好きです。
  watashi wa shodo ga suki desu

2 I LIKE…

4 minutes

Say these sentences in Japanese.

❶ I like playing tennis.
❷ I don't like football.
❸ I play baseball.
❹ I like calligraphy.

3 minutes

❸ rabbit

❻ horse

3 LEISURE

4 minutes

What do these sentences mean?

❶ **karaoke wa daikirai desu**
❷ **bideo gehmu ga suki desu**
❸ **shumi wa dokusho desu**
❹ **watashi wa gekijyoh no hohga sukidesu**
❺ **baiorin o hikimasu**

Leisure

❶ I hate karaoke.
❷ I like video games.
❸ My hobby is reading.
❹ I prefer the theatre.
❺ I play the violin.

4 AN INVITATION

4 minutes

You are invited for dinner. Join in the conversation, replying in Japanese following the numbered English prompts.

doyoh bi no dinah ni irasshai masenka
❶ Sorry, I'm busy on Saturday.

mokuyoh bi wa ikaga desuka
❷ Yes, how nice!

goshujin mo goissho ni
❸ At what time should we arrive?

ichi ji han ni
❹ Thank you very much.

An invitation

❶ すみません。
土曜日は忙しいです。
sumimasen. doyoh bi wa isogashih desu

❷ はい、楽しみです!
hai, tanoshimi desu

❸ 何時に伺いましょうか?
nanji ni ukagai mashohka

❹ ありがとうございます。
arigatoh gozaimasu

Reinforce and progress

Regular practice is the key to maintaining and advancing your language skills. In this section you will find a variety of suggestions for reinforcing and extending your knowledge of Japanese. Many involve returning to exercises in the book and extending their scope by using the dictionaries. Go back through the lessons in a different order, mix and match activities to make up your own daily 15-minute programme, or focus on topics that are of particular relevance to your current needs.

1 WARM UP

1 minute

How do you say "**I have four children**"? (pp10–11).

Say "**We're not English**" and "**I don't have a car**" (pp14–15).

What is the Japanese for "**my mother**"? (pp10–11).

Match, repeat, and extend
Remind yourself of words related to specific topics by returning to the Match and Repeat and Words to Remember exercises. Test yourself using the cover flap. Discover new words in that area by referring to the dictionary and menu guide.

Keep warmed up
Re-visit the Warm Up boxes to remind yourself of key words and phrases. Make sure you work your way through all of them on a regular basis.

2 ◄)) MATCH AND REPEAT

5 minutes

Match the numbered items to the list, then test yourself using the cover flap.

❶ 庇
hisashi

❷ 窓
mado

❸ 障子
shoji

❹ 壁
kabe

❺ 屋根
yane

❻ 階段
kaidan

❼ 雨どい
amadoi

❽ 縁側
engawa

❾ 引き戸
hikido

❿ 庭
niwa

eaves ❶   window ❷   ❸ paper window   ❹ wall   ❺ roof

steps ❻   gutter ❼   porch ❽   sliding door ❾   garden ❿

Carry on conversing
Re-read the In Conversation panels. Say both parts of the conversation, paying attention to the pronunciation. Where possible, try incorporating new words from the dictionary.

3 ◄)) IN CONVERSATION

こんにちは。岡田です。
konnichiwa. okada desu
Hello, I'm Okada.

どこで教えていらっしゃいますか？
doko de oshiete irasshai masuka
Where do you teach?

東京大学です。
tokyo daigaku desu
I teach at Tokyo University.

Practise words and phrases
Return to the Words to Remember, Useful Phrases, and Put into Practice exercises. Test yourself using the cover flap. When you are confident, devise your own versions of the phrases, using new words from the dictionary.

3 ◀)) USEFUL PHRASES

2 minutes

Learn these phrases, then test yourself using the cover flap.

今何時ですか？ **ima nanji desuka**	What time is it?
朝食は何時がいい ですか？ **chohshoku wa nanji ga iidesuka**	At what time do you want breakfast?
１２時に予約を 入れています。 **jyu-ni ji ni yoyaku o ireteimasu**	I have a reservation for twelve o'clock.

5 SAY IT

2 minutes

I'm doing research in medicine.

I have a degree in literature.

She's a professor.

Say it again
The Say It exercises are a useful instant reminder for each lesson. Practise these using your own vocabulary variations from the dictionary or elsewhere in the lesson.

1 THE BODY

4 minutes

Name these body parts in Japanese.

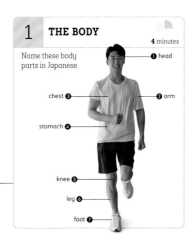

❶ head
❷ arm
chest ❸
stomach ❹
knee ❺
leg ❻
foot ❼

Review and repeat again
Work through a Review and Repeat lesson as a way of reinforcing words and phrases presented in the course. Return to the main lesson for any topic about which you are no longer confident.

Using other resources

As well as working with this book, try the following language extension ideas:

Visit Japan, if you can, and try out your new skills with native speakers. Find out if there is a Japanese community near you. There may be shops, cafés, restaurants, and clubs. Try to visit some of these and use your Japanese to order food and drink and strike up conversations. Most native speakers will be happy to speak Japanese to you.

Join a language class or club. There are usually evening and day classes available at a variety of different levels. Or you could start a club yourself if you have friends who are also interested in keeping up their Japanese.

Practise your new knowledge of the Japanese scripts and characters (see pp158–9). Look at the back of food packages and other products. You will often find a Japanese list of ingredients or components. See if you can spot some familiar words in the Japanese list and then compare to the English equivalent.

Look at the titles and advertisements of Japanese magazines and manga comics. The pictures will help you to decipher the script. Look for familiar words and characters, even if you can't make out the whole text.

Use the internet to find websites for learning languages, some of which offer free online help.

Menu guide

This guide lists the most common terms you may encounter on Japanese menus or when shopping for food. The dishes are divided into categories, and the Japanese script is given to help you identify items on a menu. If you can't find an exact phrase, try looking up its component parts.

Vegetables, soyabean products, and seasonings

アスパラ	**asupara**	asparagus
なす	**nasu**	aubergine
竹の子	**takenoko**	bamboo shoot
豆	**mame**	beans
キャベツ	**kyabetsu**	cabbage
にんじん	**ninjin**	carrot
キュウリ	**kyu-ri**	cucumber
しょうが	**shohga**	ginger
ピーマン	**pihman**	green pepper
レタス	**retasu**	lettuce
マヨネーズ	**mayonehzu**	mayonnaise
マッシュルーム	**masshurumu**	mushrooms
きのこ	**kinoko**	mushrooms (general term)
松茸	**matsutake**	mushrooms, wild (luxury ingredient)
からし	**karashi**	mustard
油	**abura**	oil
玉ねぎ	**tamanegi**	onion
ポテト／ジャガイモ	**poteto/jyagaimo**	potato
塩	**shio**	salt
塩辛い	**shiokarai**	salty
海苔	**nori**	seaweed, laver
醤油	**shoyu**	soy sauce
大豆	**daizu**	soyabean
納豆	**nattoh**	soyabeans, fermented

味噌	**miso**	soyabean paste, fermented
ほうれん草	**hohrensoh**	spinach
砂糖	**satoh**	sugar
甘い	**amai**	sweet
とうもろこし／コーン	**tohmorokoshi/kohn**	sweetcorn
豆腐	**tohfu**	tofu (bean curd)
油揚げ	**abura-age**	tofu, fried
トマト	**tomato**	tomato
野菜	**yasai**	vegetables
酢	**su**	vinegar

Soups and vegetarian dishes

おでん	**oden**	fish, meat, or vegetable hotchpotch (stew), using seaweed or fish broth, or a mix of both
サラダ	**sarada**	salad
ポテトサラダ	**poteto sarada**	salad, potato
吸い物	**suimomono**	soup, clear, made with dashi (containing kelp and fish flakes)
コーンスープ	**kohn supu**	soup, corn
ミネストローネ	**minestorohne**	soup, minestrone
みそ汁	**misoshiru**	soup, miso (fermented bean paste)
豚汁	**tonjiru/butajiru**	soup, miso, with pork and vegetables
おひたし	**ohitashi**	spinach, boiled and seasoned

Meat and poultry

牛肉／ビーフ	**gyu-niku/bihfu**	beef
鶏肉	**toriniku**	chicken
あばら肉	**abaraniku**	chops/ribs
鴨	**kamo**	duck
ひれ肉	**hireniku**	fillet
レバー	**rebah**	liver

肉	**niku**	meat
骨付き	**honetsuki**	on the bone
豚肉	**butaniku**	pork

Meat dishes

バーベキュー	**bahbekyu**	barbecue
牛しょうが焼き	**gyu-shohgayaki**	beef cooked in soy sauce with ginger
ローストビーフ	**rohsuto-bihfu**	beef, roast
しゃぶしゃぶ	**shabu-shabu**	beef, sliced, boiled with vegetables in a pot at the table
すき焼き	**sukiyaki**	beef, sliced, cooked with vegetables at the table
ビーフステーキ	**bihfu-sutehki**	beefsteak
から揚げ	**karaage**	chicken, deep fried
ローストチキン	**rohsuto-chikin**	chicken, roast
焼き鳥	**yakitori**	chicken, skewered and cooked over a grill
コロッケ	**korokke**	croquettes
ハンバーガー	**hanbahgah**	hamburger
肉団子	**nikudango**	meatballs
焼肉	**yakiniku**	meat, grilled and served with dipping sauces
串揚げ	**kushiage**	meat or vegetables on skewers, deep-fried
串焼き	**kushiyaki**	meat or vegetables on skewers, grilled
豚しょうが焼き	**buta-shohgayaki**	pork cooked in soy sauce with ginger
とんかつ	**tonkatsu**	pork cutlet, deep-fried
カツ丼	**katsudon**	pork cutlet, deep-fried, served on rice
ローストポーク	**rohsuto-pohku**	pork, roast
カレーライス	**kareh-raisu**	rice with curry-flavoured stew
ソーセージ	**sohsehji**	sausage

ステーキ	**sutehki**	steak
サーロインステーキ	**sahroin-sutehki**	steak, sirloin
スペアリブ	**spearibu**	spare ribs

Fish and shellfish

あわび	**awabi**	abalone
フグ／河豚	**fugu**	blowfish
かつお／鰹	**katsuo**	bonito, tunny
コイ／鯉	**koi**	carp
はまぐり／蛤	**hamaguri**	clam
タラ／鱈	**tara**	cod
タラコ	**tarako**	cod roe
あなご	**anago**	conger eel
かに／蟹	**kani**	crab
うなぎ／鰻	**unagi**	eel
上	**joh**	fish selection, expensive
並	**nami**	fish selection, inexpensive
にしん／鰊	**nishin**	herring
かずのこ	**kazunoko**	herring roe
あじ／鯵	**aji**	horse mackerel
伊勢えび	**ise-ebi**	lobster
さば／鯖	**saba**	mackerel
たこ／蛸	**tako**	octopus
カキ／牡蠣	**kaki**	oyster
車えび	**kuruma-ebi**	prawns
さけ／鮭	**sake**	salmon
イクラ	**ikura**	salmon roe
いわし／鰯	**iwashi**	sardines
ホタテ	**hotate**	scallop
すずき／鱸	**suzuki**	sea bass
タイ／鯛	**tai**	sea bream
うに	**uni**	sea urchin

えび／海老	**ebi**	shrimp
イカ	**ika**	squid
あゆ／鮎	**ayu**	sweet smelt
マス／鱒	**masu**	trout
まぐろ／鮪	**maguro**	tuna
くじら／鯨	**kujira**	whale
ブリ／鰤	**buri**	yellowtail

Seafood dishes

うな重	**unajyu**	eel, grilled, served on rice in a box
うな丼	**unadon**	eel, grilled, served on rice in a bowl
おでん	**oden**	fish and vegetable hotchpotch boiled in fish broth
刺身	**sashimi**	fish, raw
焼き魚	**yakizakana**	fish, grilled
スモークサーモン	**smohku sahmon**	salmon, smoked

Sushi

にぎり寿司	**nigiri-zushi**	fish, raw, on riceballs
五目寿司	**gomoku-zushi**	sushi, mixed
ちらし寿司	**chirashi-zushi**	sushi, mixed, on rice
押し寿司	**oshi-zushi**	sushi, mixed, Osaka-style and cut in squares
いなり寿司	**inari-zushi**	seasoned rice wrapped in fried tofu
カッパ巻き	**kappa-maki**	seasoned rice and cucumber rolled tightly in nori seaweed
のり巻き	**nori-maki**	seasoned rice and various ingredients rolled tightly in nori seaweed

Egg dishes

茶碗蒸し	**chawan-mushi**	custard made with steamed egg, savoury
卵	**tamago**	egg
ベーコンエッグ	**behkon-eggu**	egg and bacon
ハムエッグ	**hamu-eggu**	egg and ham
目玉焼き	**medama-yaki**	egg, fried
卵豆腐	**tamago-dohfu**	egg tofu, steamed (without soyabeans)
オムレツ	**omuretsu**	omelette
卵焼き	**tamago-yaki**	omelette, Japanese
オムライス	**omuraisu**	omelette, rolled, filled with rice

Rice dishes

…丼	**…donburi**	bowl of rice with something on top
卵丼	**tamagodon**	donburi cooked in egg with onions
親子丼	**oyakodon**	donburi with chicken and egg
カツ丼	**katsudon**	donburi with deep-fried breaded pork cutlet
天丼	**tendon**	donburi with deep-fried seafood
中華丼	**chyukadon**	donburi with pork and vegetables
牛丼	**gyudon**	donburi with sliced beef
おもち／もち	**omochi/mochi**	mochi (rice cake), soft and glutinous when ready to eat
ご飯／ライス	**gohan/raisu**	rice
チャーハン	**chah-han**	rice, fried
おにぎり	**onigiri**	rice shaped into a triangle, round, or oval with various ingredients inside, rolled tightly in nori seaweed
釜飯	**kamameshi**	rice steamed in fish stock with pieces of meat, fish, and vegetable
チキンライス	**chikin raisu**	rice with chicken

Noodle dishes

ラーメン	**ramen**	noodles, Chinese
焼きそば	**yakisoba**	noodles, Chinese, fried
ちゃんぽん	**chanpon**	noodles, Chinese, in salted stock, with meat and vegetables
そうめん	**sohmen**	noodles, long, thin, made of white wheat flour, usually served cold in the summer
ワンタンメン	**wantan-men**	ramen and dumplings (wantan) containing ground pork and leeks, served in soup
味噌ラーメン	**miso ramen**	ramen in miso-flavoured broth
広東麺	**kanton-men**	ramen in salted pork-flavoured soup with vegetables
五目そば	**gomoku soba**	ramen or soba in broth with pieces of vegetable and meat
もやしそば	**moyashi soba**	ramen with bean sprouts
チャーシューメン	**chahshumen**	ramen with grilled pork
そば	**soba**	soba noodles, long, brownish, made of buckwheat
かけそば	**kake soba**	soba in fish broth
月見そば	**tsukimi soba**	soba in fish broth with an egg
きつねうどん	**kitsune udon**	soba in fish broth with fried tofu
力うどん	**chikara udon**	soba in fish broth with mochi (rice cake)
盛りそば	**mori soba**	soba served cold, with sweetened soy sauce dip
天ぷらそば	**tempura soba**	soba with deep-fried shrimps
うどん	**udon**	udon noodles, long, thick, made of white wheat flour
肉うどん	**niku udon**	udon in fish stock with pork or beef

Japanese set meals

弁当	**bento**	boxed lunch
定食	**teishoku**	set meal with rice, soup, pickle, and main dish
日替わり定食	**higawari teishoku**	teishoku of the day
とんかつ定食	**tonkatsu teishoku**	teishoku with battered and deep-fried pork cutlet as the main dish
から揚げ定食	**karaage teishoku**	teishoku with deep-fried chicken as a main dish
天ぷら定食	**tempura teishoku**	teishoku with deep-fried prawns, seafood, or vegetables as the main dish
焼肉定食	**yakiniku teishoku**	teishoku with grilled meat as the main dish
刺身定食	**sashimi teishoku**	teishoku with raw fish as the main dish

Chinese meals

中華料理	**chu-ka ryohri**	Chinese food
餃子	**gyohza**	dumpling, fried, stuffed with minced pork
シュウマイ	**shu-mai**	dumpling, small, steamed, made of thin Chinese filo pastry filled with pork
肉まん	**nikuman**	dumpling, steamed, filled with seasoned minced pork
くらげ	**kurage**	jellyfish, sliced and parboiled
酢豚	**subuta**	pork, sweet-and-sour
春巻き	**harumaki**	spring roll, deep-fried
マーボー豆腐	**mahboh-dohfu**	tofu in spicy meat sauce mixture

Izakaya menu

おつまみ	**otsumami**	appetizers and finger foods served at izakaya
お通し／つきだし	**otohshi/tsukidashi**	appetizers and small nibbles served at izakaya as a "cover charge" dish
枝豆	**edamame**	beans, green, in the pod, served as snacks with drinks
ハム	**hamu**	ham
オードブル	**ohdoburu**	hors d'oeuvres
タクアン	**takuan**	radish, yellow, pickled

Street food

綿菓子	**watagashi**	candy floss
甘栗	**amaguri**	chestnut, roasted
焼きとうもろこし	**yaki tohmorokoshi**	corn on the cob, roasted
たこ焼き	**takoyaki**	octopus, griddle-fried in batter
お好み焼き	**okonomiyaki**	pancake, savoury, Japanese-style
焼き芋	**yaki-imo**	sweet potato, baked
イカ焼き	**ikayaki**	squid, charcoal-grilled

Western snacks

パン	**pan**	bread
バター	**batah**	butter
フライドチキン	**furaido chikin**	chicken, fried
ハムサンド	**hamusando**	ham sandwich
ジャム	**jamu**	jam
マーマレード	**mahmarehdo**	marmalade
ピザ	**piza**	pizza
サンドイッチ	**sando icchi**	sandwich
スパゲッティ	**spagetti**	spaghetti
トースト	**tohsuto**	toast

Fruit and nuts

バナナ	**banana**	banana
チェリー／さくらんぼ	**cherih/sakuranbo**	cherry
栗	**kuri**	chestnut
ココナッツ	**kokonattsu**	coconut
フルーツ／果物	**furu-tsu/kudamono**	fruit
グレープフルーツ	**gurehpu furu-tsu**	grapefruit
レモン	**remon**	lemon
メロン	**meron**	melon
オレンジ	**orenji**	orange
ピーチ／桃	**pihchi/momo**	peach
柿	**kaki**	persimmon
パイナップル	**painappuru**	pineapple
ラズベリー／木苺	**razuberih/kiichigo**	raspberry
みかん	**mikan**	satsuma
ストロベリー／イチゴ	**sutoroberih/ichigo**	strawberry
クルミ	**kurumi**	walnut
スイカ	**suika**	watermelon

Desserts

おしるこ	**oshiruko**	bean soup, sweet, with mochi (rice cake)
ケーキ	**kehki**	cake
チーズケーキ	**chihzu kehki**	cheesecake
チョコレート	**chokorehto**	chocolate
シュークリーム	**shu-kurihmu**	cream puff
クレープ	**kurehpu**	crêpe
プリン	**purin**	custard pudding (crème caramel)
デザート	**dezahto**	dessert
ドーナツ	**dohnatsu**	doughnut
みつ豆	**mitsumame**	gelatine cubes and sweet beans with pieces of fruit

アイスクリーム	**aisukurihmu**	ice cream
ストロベリー アイスクリーム	**sutoroberih aisukurihmu**	ice cream, strawberry
バニラ アイスクリーム	**banira aisukurihmu**	ice cream, vanilla
クリームあんみつ	**kurihmu anmitsu**	ice cream, vanilla, with seaweed jelly, sweet beans, and fruit
かき氷	**kaki gohri**	ice, shaved, with various sweet toppings, popular in summer
ゼリー	**zerih**	jelly
ようかん	**yohkan**	jelly with soft, sweet bean paste filling
大福	**daifuku**	mochi (rice cake), small and round, stuffed with sweet fillings such as red bean paste
アップルパイ	**appuru pai**	pie, apple
せんべい	**senbeh**	rice cracker
まんじゅう	**manjyu**	rice-flour bun with bean paste
ショートケーキ	**shohto kehki**	"shortcake" (similar to sponge cake)
シャーベット	**shahbetto**	sorbet
スフレ	**sufure**	soufflé
カステラ	**kasutera**	sponge cake
ヨーグルト	**yohguruto**	yoghurt

Alcoholic drinks

ビール	**bihru**	beer
生ビール	**nama bihru**	beer, draught
お酒／日本酒	**osake/nihonshu**	rice wine
焼酎	**shohchuh**	spirit distilled from a variety of raw materials, including rice, barley, buckwheat, and sweet potatoes
ウイスキー	**uisukih**	whisky
オンザロック	**onzarokku**	(whisky) on the rocks
水割り	**mizuwari**	(whisky) with water
ワイン／ぶどう酒	**wain/budohshu**	wine

Non-alcoholic drinks

飲み物	**nomimono**	beverages, drinks
ココア	**kokoa**	cocoa, hot chocolate
コーヒー	**koh-hi**	coffee
コーラ	**kohra**	cola
サイダー	**saidah**	fizzy drink
オレンジジュース	**orenji jyu-su**	juice, orange
パインジュース	**pain jyu-su**	juice, pineapple
トマトジュース	**tomato jyu-su**	juice, tomato
ミルク／牛乳	**miruku/gyu-nyu**	milk
ミルクシェイク	**miruku shehku**	milkshake
ミネラル ウォーター	**mineraru wohtah**	mineral water
オレンジ スカッシュ	**orenji sukasshu**	orange drink, fizzy
ソーダ水	**sohda sui**	soda water
紅茶	**kohcha**	tea, black (literally *red tea*)
お茶／緑茶／煎茶	**ocha/ryokucha/sencha**	tea, Japanese
レモンティー	**remon tih**	tea, lemon
ミルクティー	**miruku tih**	tea with milk
トニック ウォーター	**tonikku wohtah**	tonic water

Methods of preparation

ゆでた	**yudeta**	boiled
炉端焼き	**robatayaki**	charcoal-grilled fish and vegetables
お菓子	**okashi**	confectionery
揚げ物	**agemono**	deep-fried foods
天ぷら	**tenpura**	deep-fried seafood and vegetables in batter
鍋物	**nabemono**	food cooked in a pot at the table
揚げた	**ageta**	fried
焼いた	**yaita**	grilled
焼き物	**yakimono**	grilled foods
懐石料理	**kaiseki ryohri**	Japanese multicourse meals
日本食／和食	**nihon shoku/washoku**	Japanese-style cuisine
鉄板焼き	**teppan-yaki**	meat/fish/vegetables grilled on an iron plate at the table
麺類	**men rui**	noodle dishes
漬物	**tsukemono**	pickled foods
鳥料理	**tori-ryohri**	poultry dishes
生の	**nama no**	raw
郷土料理	**kyohdo ryohri**	regional specialities
ご飯もの	**gohan-mono**	rice dishes
ローストした	**rohsuto shita**	roasted
煮た	**nita**	simmered
煮物	**nimono**	simmered foods
汁物	**shirumono**	soups
割烹	**kappoh**	special order Japanese-style dishes
蒸した	**mushita**	steamed
蒸し物	**mushimono**	steamed foods
精進料理	**shohjin ryohri**	ascetic, monastic style of vegetarian cooking
酢の物	**sunomono**	vinegared foods
西洋料理	**sehyoh ryohri**	Western-style cuisine

Dictionary
ENGLISH TO JAPANESE

The plural is normally the same as the singular in Japanese. In general, Japanese descriptive words, or adjectives, may change depending on how they are used. Some of these adjectives are followed by **no** or **na**. If a noun is used following such a word then the **no** or **na** must be put after the adjective: **kanojo wa kireh desu** (*she is pretty*) but **kanojo wa kireh na jyoseh desu** (*she is a pretty girl*). Adjectives and verbs are denoted by *adj* and *verb*.

A

about: about 16 **jyu-roku kurai**
accelerator **akuseru**
access **akusesu**
accident **jiko**
accommodation **shukuhaku shisetsu**
accountant **kaikehshi**
ache (verb) **itamu**
actor **haiyuu**
adapter (electrical) **adaputa**
address **jyu-sho**
adjectives **keiyoh-shi**
admission charge **nyujoh ryoh**
aeroplane **hikohki**
after **ato**
afternoon **gogo**
aftershave lotion **afutah-shehbu-rohshon**
again **mata**
against **hantai**
agenda **kaigi jikoh, ajenda**
agent (rental) **fudohsanya**
agree (verb) **sansei suru**
air conditioning **eakon**
air freshener **ea-furesshnah**
airline **kohku-gaisha**
air mail **ea mehru**
airport **ku-koh**
alcohol **arukohru**; *alcoholic drinks* **osake**
all **zenbu**; *that's all, thanks* **arigatoh, sore de zenbu desu**
allergy **arerugih**
almost **hotondo**
alone (adj) **hitori de**
already **sudeni**
always **itsumo**
am: I am British **watashi wa igirisu jin desu**
ambulance **kyu-kyu-sha**
America **amerika**
American (person) **amerika jin**; (adj) **amerika no**
and (with nouns) **to**; (with verbs) **soshite**
animal **dohbutsu**
ankle **ashikubi**
anniversary **kinenbi**; *wedding anniversary* **kekkon kinenbi**
anorak **anorakku**
another (different) **betsu (no)**; (further) **moh hitotsu (no)**

answering machine **rusuban denwa**
antifreeze **futohzai**
antique shop **kottoh hin ten**
antiseptic **bohfuzai, shohdokuzai**
apartment (flat) **aparto**; *apartment* (luxury) **manshon**
appetite **shokuyoku**
appetizer **otsumami, otoshi/ tsukidashi**
apple **ringo**; (pie) **appuru pie**
application form **mohshikomisho**
appointment **(go)yoyaku; apo**
apricot **anzu**
April **shi gatsu**
architecture (field of study) **kenchiku gaku**
are: you are very kind **anata wa totemo shinsetsu desu**; *we are English* **watashi tachi wa igirisu jin desu**; *they are Japanese* **karera wa nihonjin desu**
arm **ude**
armchair **hijikake isu/ ahmu chea**
arrivals **tohchaku**
art **ahto; bijutsu/geijyutsu**
art gallery **bijutsukan**
artist **geijyutsuka**
as: as soon as possible **dekiru dake hayaku**
ashtray **haizara**
Asia **Ajia**
asleep (adj): *he's asleep* **kare wa nemutte imasu**
asthmatic (adj): *I'm asthmatic* **zensoku mochi desu**
aspirin **asupirin**
at: at the post office **yu-bin kyoku de**; *at night* **yoru**; *at 3 o'clock* **san ji ni**
attic **yane ura**
attractive (adj) **miryokuteki (na)**
August **hachi gatsu**
aunt **oba(san)**; *my aunt* **oba**
Australia **Ohsutoraria**
Australian (person) **ohsutoraria jin**; (adj) **ohsutoraria no**
automatic (adj) **jidoh**
autumn **aki**
away: is it far away? **tohi desuka**; *go away!* **atchi e itte**

awful (adj) **hidoi**
axe **ono**
axle **shajiku**

B

B&B (family run) **minshuku**
baby **akachan**
baby wipes **bebih waipu**
bachelor's **gakushi**
back **ushiro**; (upper back, body) **senaka**; (lower back, body) **koshi**
bacon **behkon**; *bacon and eggs* **behkon-eggu**
bad (adj) **warui**
bag **kaban; fukuro**
baggage **nimotsu**
baker **pan ya**
balcony **barukonih**
ball **bohru**; (dance) **butohkai**
ball-point pen **bohru-pen**
banana **banana**
band (musicians) **bando**
bandage **hohtai**
bank **ginkoh**
banknotes **shiheh**
bar **bah**; *bar of chocolate* **itachoko**
barber **toko ya**
barbecue **bahbekyu**
bargain **bahgen**
baseball **yakyu**; *baseball bat* **batto**; *baseball player* **yakyu senshu**
basement **chika**
basin (sink) **sen-mendai**
basket **kago**
bath **ofuro**; *to have a bath* (verb) **ofuro ni hairu**; (outdoor, onsen) **roten buro**
bathhouse **sento**
bathing hat **sui-ei boh**
bathroom **basu ru-mu; ofuroba**
battery **batteri; denchi**
beach **hamabe, kaigan**
beans **mame**
beard **ago hige**
beautiful (adj) **utsukushih**
beauty products **keshoh hin**
because **(da)kara**; *because it is too big* **ohki-sugiru kara**
bed **beddo**
bed linen **shihtsu to makurakabah**

bedroom **shinshitsu, beddo ru-mu**
bedside table **beddo saido tehburu**
bedspread **beddo supureddo**
beef **gyu-niku, bihfu**; *beefsteak* **bihfu-sutehki**
beer **bihru**
before **mae ni**
beginner **shoshinsha**
behind **ushiro**
beige (adj) **behju**
bell **beru**
below **shita**
belt **beruto**
beside **soba**
best (adj) **ichiban ih**
better (adj) **motto ih**
between **aida ni**
beverage (drinks) **nomimono**
bicycle **jitensha**
big (adj) **ohkih**
bikini **bikini**
bill **okanjoh**
biochemistry **seikagaku**
bird **tori**
birthday **tanjyobi**; *happy birthday!* **otanjyohbi omedetoh**; *birthday present* **tanjyohbi no purezento**
biscuit **bisuketto**
bite (verb) **kamu**; (by insect) **mushi sasare**
bitter (adj) **nigai**
black (adj) **kuroi**; **kuro**
blanket **mohfu**
blind (cannot see) **mohmoku (no)** (on window) **buraindo**
blister **mizu-bukure**
blood **ketsueki, chi**; *blood test* **ketsueki kensa**
blouse **burausu**
blow: to blow (wind instruments) (verb) **fukimasu**
blue **ao**; (adj) **aoi**
boarding pass **tohjyoh ken**
boarding gate **tohjyoh guchi**
boat **fune**
body **karada**
boil (verb: water) **wakasu**: on body) **hare-mono**
boiled (adj) **yudeta**
bolt (on door) **boruto**
bone **hone**
bonnet (car) **bon-netto**
bonsai **bonsai**
book **hon**; (verb) **yoyaku suru**; *bookshop* **hon ya**
booking office **kippu uriba**
boot (car) **toranku**; (footwear) **bu-tsu**
border **kokkyoh**
boring (adj) **tsumaranai**
born (verb): *I was born in...* (place) **watashi wa... de umare-mashita**; (year) **watashi wa... nen ni umare-mashita**
both **ryohhoh**; *both of them* **futari tomo**; *both of us* **watashi tachi**

futari; *both... and... ...to...*
bottle **bin**
bottle opener **sennuki**
bottom (of box, sea) **soko**
bow **ojigi**
bowl **bohru**; **chawan**
box **hako**
boxed lunch **bento**
boy **otoko no ko**
boyfriend **bohi-furendo**
bra **burajah**
bracelet **udewa, buresuretto**
braces (trousers) **zubon-tsuri**
brake **burehki**; (verb) **burehki o kakeru**
branch (office) **shiten**
brandy **burandeh**
bread **pan**
breakdown (car) **koshoh**; (nervous) **shinkei-suijaku**
breakfast **chohshoku**
breathe (verb) **iki o suru**; *I can't breathe* **iki ga dekimasen**
breathless **iki ga kurushih**
bricklayer **burokkukoh**
bridge **hashi**
briefcase **kaban**
British (things) **igirisu no**; (adj) *the British* **igirisu jin**
brochure **panfuretto**
broken (adj) **kowareta**; *broken leg* **kossetsu shita ashi**; (verb) *... is broken* **...ga kowarete imasu**
brooch **burohchi**
brother (older) **onihsan**; (older, my) **ani**; (younger) **otohto**
brown (adj) **cha-iro (no)**
bruise **dabokushoh, uchimi**
brush **burashi**
bucket **baketsu**
Buddha **Hotoke**
Buddhism **Bukkyoh**
Buddhist **Bukkyohto**; (adj) **Bukkyoh no**
budget **yosan**
builder **kenchiku ka**
building **tatemono, biru**
bumper **banpah**
bunker **bankah**
burglar **doroboh, yatoh**
burn (verb) **moyasu**; **yakedo**
bus **basu**
business **shigoto; bijinesu**
businessman **kaisha in**
business card **meishi**
bushes **teiboku**
bus station **basu tahminaru**
bus stop **basu teh**
busy (adj) (person) **isogashih**; (crowded) **konzatsu shita**
but **demo**
butcher **niku ya**
butter **batah**
button **botan**
buy (verb) **kau**
by: by the window **mado no soba**
by Friday **kinyohbi ma-de ni** *by myself* **jibun de**

C

cabbage **kyabetsu**
cabinet (kitchen) **todana**
cable car **kehburu kah**
cable TV **kehbru terebi**
café (Western) **kafe, kissaten**; (Japanese teahouse) **chaya, chamise**
cake **kehki**; *cake shop* **kehki ya**; (sponge cake) **kasutera**
calculator **kehsanki**
call (verb): *what's it called?* **nan to ihmasuka**
calligraphy **shodo**
came (verb, past) **kimashita**
camera **kamera**
can (tin) **kanzume**; *can I have...?* **...o onegai shimasu**
Canada **Kanada**
Canadian (person) **kanada jin**; (adj) **kanada no**
cancer **gan**
candle **rohsoku**
candy floss **watagashi**
canopy **hisashi**
cap (bottle) **futa**; (hat) **bohshi**
capsule hotels **kapuseruhoteru**
car **kuruma**; (small car) **chihsai kuruma**
car park **chusha jyo**
carburettor **kyaburetah**
card (business) **meishi**
cardigan **kahdigan**
careful (adj) **chu-i-bukai**; *be careful!* **ki o tsukete**
carpenter **daiku**
carpet **jyu-tan, kahpetto**
carriage (train) **kyakusha**
carrot **ninjin**
carry-cot **akachan yoh kehtai beddo**
car seat (for a baby) **bebih shihto**
case (suitcase) **su-tsu-kehsu**
cash (money) **genkin**; (coins) **kohka, koin** *to pay cash* **genkin de harau**
cashier (for bank) **modoguchi**; (for shop/restaurant) **reji**
cashpoint **"ATM"**
cassette **kasetto**
cassette player **kasetto purehyah**
castle **shiro**
cat **neko**
cave **hora-ana, dohkutsu**
CD drive **CD doraibu**
ceiling **ten-jyoh**
cemetery **bochi**
centre **sentah**
certificate **shohmeisho**
chair **isu**; *swivel chair* **kaiten isu**
chambermaid **meido**
change (money) **otsuri**; (verb: general) **kaeru**; (verb:transport) **norikaeru**
changing room **datsuijo**
character (written) **ji**

charger (electrical) **chahjyah**; (car) **jyuhdenki**

charging point **jyuhden sutando**;

charging station **jyuhden sutehshon**

charging cable **jyuhden kehburu**

cheap (adj) **yasui**

check-in **chekku in**; *check-in counter* **chekku in kauntah**

check-out (hotel) **chekku auto**; (supermarket) **reji**

cheers! **kanpai**

cheese **chihzu**

cheesecake **chihzu kehki**

chemist (shop) **yakkyoku, kusuriya**

cheque **kogitte**

cheque book **kogitte choh**

cherry **sakuranbo, cherih**

chess **chesu**

chest **mune**

chest of drawers **tansu**

chestnut **kuri**; (roasted) **amaguri**

chewing gum **chu-in-gamu**

chicken (meat) **toriniku**; (bird) **niwatori**; *fried chicken* **furaido chikin**

child **kodomo**

children **kodomotachi**; *children's ward* **shohni byohtoh**

china **tohki**

China **chu-goku**

Chinese (person) **chu-goku jin**; (adj) **chu-goku no**

Chinese food **chu-ka ryohri**

chips **furaido poteto**

chocolate **chokorehto**; *box of chocolates* **hakozume no chokorehto**

chop (food) **choppu**; (verb: to cut) **kizamu**

chopstick rest **hashi oki**

chopsticks **ohashi**

Christian name **namae**

Christmas **kurisumasu**

church **kyohkai**

cigar **hamaki**

cigarette **tabako**

cinema **eiga**; *cinema* (place) **eigakan**

city **toshi, machi**

city centre **chu shingai**

class: (adj: train) *first class carriage* **ittoh sha**; *second class carriage* **nitoh sha**

classical music **kurasshikku ongaku**

clean (adj) **kireh (na)**; (verb) **sohji suru**

cleaning staff **seisoh gyohsha**

clear (adj) (obvious) **meihaku (na)**; *is that clear?* **wakari-masuka**; (water) **sumikitta**

clever (adj) **kashikoi**

client **kokyaku**

wall clock **tokei** (alarm) **mezamashi-dokei**

clogs **geta**

close (adj) (near) **chikai**; (stuffy) **iki-gurushih**; (verb) **shimeru**; *we close at six o'clock* **roku ji ni shimarimasu**

clothes **fuku**

clothes size **fuku no saizu**

club **kurabu**; (cards) **kurabu**

coach **choh-kyori basu**; (of train) **kyakusha**; *coach station* **basu hacchaku jyo**

coat **kohto**

cocoa (hot chocolate) **kokoa**

coathanger **hangah**

cockroach **gokiburi**

coffee **koh-hi**; *black coffee* **burakku koh-hi**

coins **kohka, koin**

cold (adj) (illness) **kaze**; (weather) **samui**; (food, material, etc) **tsumetai**

collar **eri**

collar (for pets) **kubiwa**

collection (stamps, etc) **shu-shu**

colour **iro**

colour film **karah firumu**

comb **kushi** (verb) **toku**

come (verb) **kuru/kimasu**; *coming* **kimasu**; *come to my party* **pahtih ni kitene**; *come here!* **koko ni kinasai**; *I come from... ...kara kimashita*; *come!* (invitation) **kite**

company **kaisha**

compartment **shikiri kyakushitsu**

complicated (adj) **fukuzatsu (na)**

computer **konpyu-tah**; *computer repair shop* **konpyu-tah shu-ri ten**; *computer repairman* **konpyu-tah shu-ri-koh**

concert **ongakukai, konsahto**

condition **guai**

conditioner (hair) **rinsu, kondishonah**

conductor (orchestra) **shikisha**

confectionery (snacks) **okashi**; (category) **kashi rui**

conference (meeting) **konfarensu**; (academic) **gakkai**

congratulations! **omedetoh**

constipation **benpi**

consul **ryohji**

consulate **ryohjikan**

consultant **consarutanto**

contact lenses **kontakuto renzu**

contactless payment **kontakutoresu kessai**

contraceptive (pills) **hinin-yaku**; (device) **hiningu, kondohmu**

contract **kehyaku sho**

convenience stores **konbini**

conversion plug **henkan puragu**

cook (person) **kokku**; (verb) **ryohri suru**

cooking utensils **ryohri-dohgu**

cool (adj) **suzushih**

cork **koruku**

corkscrew **sen-nuki**

corner **kado**

corridor **rohka**

cosmetics **keshohhin**

cost (verb) **kakaru**; *what does it cost?* **ikura kakari-masuka**

cotton **men, kotton**

cotton wool **dasshimen**

cough **seki**

country (state) **kuni**; (not town) **inaka**

cousin **itoko**

cow **ushi**

crab **kani**

cramp **keiren**

crayfish **zarigani**

cream (for face; food) **kurihmu**

cream puff **shu-kurihmu**

credit card **kurejitto kahdo**

crêpe **kurehpu**

crime **hanzai**

crisps **poteto chippusu**

crossing (pedestrian) **ohdan hodoh**

croquette **korokke**

crowded (adj) **konzatsu shita**

cruise **kohkai, kuru-zu**

crutches **matsubazue**

cry (verb) (weep) **naku**; (shout) **sakebu**

cucumber **kyuri**

cuff links **kafusu botan**

cup **kappu**

cupboard **todana**

curlers **kahrah**

curry **kareh**

curtains **kahten**

cushion **kusshon**

customs **zeikan**

cut **kirikizu** (verb) **kiru**

cycling **saikuringu**

D

dad **otohsan**

dairy (products) **nyu seihin**

damp (adj) **shimetta**

dance (verb) **dansu**

dangerous (adj) **abunai**

dark (adj) **kurai**

date **nichi**

daughter **musume san**; *my daughter* **musume**

day **hizuke, hi**; *day of the week* **yohbi**

dead (adj) **shinda**

deaf (adj) **mimi ga tohi**

dear (adj) (person) **shitashih**; (expensive) **takai**

December **jyu-ni gatsu**

deck chair **dekki che-ah**

decorator **tosohkoh**

degree (education) **gakui**

deep (adj) **fukai**

delayed **okurete**

deliberately **wazato**

delicatessen **derikatessen**

delivery **haitatsu**

dentist **ha-isha**

dentures **ireba**
deodorant **deodoranto**
department (of company, etc) **bu**
department store **depahto**
departures **shuppatsu**
deposit (long-term rental) **shikikin**
describe (verb) **setsumei suru**
description **setsumei**
designer **dezainah**
desk **tsukue, desuku**
dessert **dezahto**
detached house **ikkenya**
develop (verb) (a film)
    genzoh suru
diabetic (adj): *I'm diabetic*
    tohnyoh byoh desu
diamond (jewel) **daiyamondo**;
    (cards) **daiya**
diarrhoea **geri**
diary (record of past events) **nikki**;
    (schedule) **techoh**
dictionary **jisho**
didn't come (verb, past negative)
    kimasen deshita
die (verb) **shinu**
diesel **dihzeru**
different (adj) **chigau, betsu**
    (**no**); *I'd like a different*
    one **betsu no ga hoshih desu**
difficult (adj) **muzukashih**
dining car **shokudohsha**
dining room **dainingu ru-mu,**
    shokudoh; (with kitchen)
    dainingu kicchin
dining table (low) **chabudai**
dinner **yu-shoku, dinah**
dinner party **dinah pahtih**
directory (telephone) **denwachoh**
dirty (adj) **kitanai**
disabled (adj) **karada no**
    fujiyu (**na**)
discount **waribiki**
dishwasher **shokki araiki**
dive (verb) **tobikomu**
diving board **tobikomi-dai**
divorced (adj) **rikonshita**
do (verb) **suru**; *to do* (verb)
    shimasu
doctor **isha**
document **shohsho,**
    dokyumento, shorui
dog **inu**
doll **nin-gyoh**
dollar **doru**
door **doa**; *sliding* **hikido**
double room (hotel) **daburu**
    ru-mu; (ryokan) **hutari-beya**
doughnut **dohnatsu**
down **shita**
drawer **hikidashi**
drawing pin **oshi pin**
dress **doresu**
drink (verb) **nomu;** (beverage)
    nomimono
drinking water **nomimizu**
drive (verb) **untensuru**
driver **untenshu**
driving licence **unten menkyosho**

drops (for eyes) **megusuri**
drug store **yakkyoku, kusuriya**
drums **doramu**
dry (adj) **kawaita**
dry cleaner **dorai kurihningu ya**
duck **kamo**
dummy (for baby) **oshaburi**
*during: during... ...no aida ni**
dustbin **gomibako**
duster **dasutah**
duty-free **menzei**
duvet **kakebuton**

E

each (every) **sorezore**; *200 yen*
    each **sorezore ni-hyaku**
    en desu
ear **mimi**
early (adj) **hayai**
earphones **iyafon**
earrings **iyaringu**
east **higashi**
easy (adj) **yasashih,**
    kantan (**na**)
eat (verb) **taberu**
editor **henshuhsha**
egg **tamago**; (fried) **medama-yaki**
eight (adj, numeral) **hachi**; *eight*
    people (classifier) **hachi nin**
eighteen (adj) **jyu-hachi**
eighty (adj) **hachi-jyu**
either: either of them **dochira**
    demo; *either... or...* **...ka...**
elastic **gomuhimo**
elastic band **wagomu**
elbow **hiji**
electric (adj) **denki no**
electrician **denki gishi**
electricity **denki**
electronics **denshi-kohgaku**
electronics store **denkiya**
eleven (adj) **jyu-ichi**
else: something else **nanika**
    hokano mono; *someone else*
    dareka hokano hito; *anything*
    else? **nanika hoka ni**
email (ih) **mehru**; *email address*
    (ih) **mehru adoresu**
embarrassing (adj) **hazukashih**
embassy **taishikan**
embroidery **shishuh**
emerald **emerarudo**; (adj)
    emerarudo no
emergency **hijoh** *emergency ward*
    kyu-kyu byohtoh
emperor **tennoh**
empty (adj) **kara** (**no**)
end **owari**
engaged (adj) (couple) **konyaku**
    shita; (telephone) **hanashichu**
engine (motor) **enjin**
engineering (field of study)
    kohgaku
engineer **enjinia**
England **igirisu**
English (adj) **igirisu no**

(language) **eigo**
English person **igirisu jin**
enlargement (of photography)
    hikinobashi
enough **jyu-bun**
entertainment **goraku**
entrance **nyu-jyoh guchi, iriguchi**
entrance ticket **nyu-jyo ken**
envelope **fu-toh**
epileptic (adj): *I'm epileptic* **tenkan**
    mochi desu
escalator **esukarehtah**
especially **tokuni**
estimate **mitsumori**
Europe **Yohroppa**
evening **yu-gata, yoru**;
    good evening **konbanwa**
every (morning, day, etc) **mai-**;
    (all) **subete no**
everyone **minna**
everything **minna, zenbu**
everywhere **doko demo**
executive (person) **jyu-yaku**
exhibition **tenji kai**
examine **kensa**
example **rei**; *for example* **tatoeba**
excellent (adj) **saikoh, subarashih**
excess baggage **chohka-nimotsu**
exchange (verb) (money) **ryogae**
    suru; *can I exchange this?*
    kohkan dekimasuka
exchange rate **ryogae rehto**
excursion (school) **ensoku**;
    (sightseeing) **kankoh ryokoh**
excuse me! **shitsurei**
    shimasu, sumimasen
exhaust (car) **eguzohsuto**
exit **deguchi**
expensive (adj) **takai**
express train **kyuko, tokkyu**
explain (verb) **setsumei suru**
extension (telephone) **naisen**;
    (lengthening) **kakuchoh**
eye **me**
eyebrow **mayu**
eyewitness **mokugeki sha**

F

face **kao**
face mask **masuku**
faint (unclear) **usui, bonyari shita**;
    (verb) **kizetsu suru**; *to feel faint*
    memai ga suru
fair (funfair) **yu-enchi**; *it's not fair*
    fukohhei desu
false teeth **ireba, gishi**
family **kazoku**
fan (folding fan) **sensu**; (electric)
    senpu-ki; (enthusiast) **fan**
fan belt **fan beruto**
far (adj) **toh-i**; *is it far from here?*
    koko kara toh-i desuka
Far East **Kyokutoh**
fare **unchin**; **ryohkin**
farm **nohjoh**
farmer **nohfu**

fashion **fasshon**

fast (adj) **hayai**

fat (adj) (of person) **futotta**; (on meat, etc) **abura, shiboh**

father **otohsan**; *my father* **chichi**; *my father-in-law* **giri no chichi**

February **ni gatsu**

feel (verb) (touch) **sawaru**; *I feel hot* **atsui desu**; *I feel like... ...no yoh na ki ga shimasu**

felt-tip pen **feruto pen**

ferry **ferih**

fever **netsu**

fiancé(e) **konyakusha, fianse**

field (agricultural) **hatake**; *what's your field?* **gosenmon wa**

fifteen (adj) **jyu-go**

fifty (adj) **go-jyu**

fig **ichijiku**

figures (sales, etc) **gohkeh gaku, suhji**

fill **umeru**

fillet **hireniku**

filling (tooth) **ha no jyu-ten**; (sandwich) **nakami**

film (cinema) **eiga**; (camera) **firumu**

filter **firutah**

finger **yubi**

fire **hi**; (blaze) **honoh**

fire extinguisher **shohkaki**

fire service **shohboh-sha**

firework **hanabi**

first **saisho** (no)

first aid **ohkyu teate**

first floor **ikkai**

fish **sakana**

fishing **sakana tsuri**; *to go fishing* **tsuri ni iku**; *fishing rod* **tsuri zao**

fishmonger **sakana ya**

five (adj, numeral) **go**; *five people* (classifier) **go nin**; *five minutes* **go fun**; *five past ten* **ichi ji go fun**

fizzy (adj) **tansan no**

flag **hata; furaggu**

flash (camera) **furasshu**

flat (adj: level) **taira (na)**; (apartment) **apahto**

flat tyre **panku**

flavour **aji**

flea **nomi**

flight **hikoh(ki)**; *flight number... ...bin*; *flight attendant* **kyakushitsu jyohmuin, furaito atendanto**

flip-flops **zohri, sandaru**

flippers **ashi hire**

floor (of room) **yuka**

floor cushion **zabuton**

florist **hana ya**

flour **komugiko**

flower **hana**

flute **furu-to**

fly (verb) **tobu**; (insect) **hae**

flyover **rittai kohsa**

fog **kiri**

folk music **minzoku ongaku, fohku myu-jikku**

folk art **mingei**; (section in department stores) **kyohdo zaiku**

food **tabemono**; (deep-fried) **agemono**; (grilled) **yakimono**; (regional specialities) **kyohdo ryohri**

food poisoning **shoku chuhdoku**

food tours (walking) **tabe-aruki**

food truck **kicchin cah**

foot (on body) **ashi**

football **sakkah** (ball) **bohru**

fond **suki**

for: for... ...no tame ni; *for me* **watashi no tame ni**; *what for?* **nan no tame ni**; *for a week* **isshu-kan**

foreigner **gaikoku jin**

forest **mori**

forest bathing **shinrin-yoku**

fork **fohku**

fortnight **ni-shu-kan**

forty (adj) **yon-jyu**

fountain **funsui**

fountain pen **mannen-hitsu**

four (adj, numeral) **shi, yon**; *four people* (classifier) **yo nin**

four seasons **shinkashuto**

fourteen (adj) **jyu-yon, jyu-shi**

fourth **yonbanme**

fracture **kossetsu**

free (adj) **jiyu (na)**; (no cost) **muryoh**

free entrance **nyu-jyo muryoh**

freezer **reitohko**

Friday **kinyohbi**

fridge **reizohko**

fried (adj) **ageta**

friend **tomodachi**

friendly (adj) **shitashimi no aru, furendorih na**

front: in front of... ...no mae ni

front desk **furonto desuku**

frost **shimo**

frozen foods **reitoh shokuhin**

fruit **kudamono, furu-tsu**

fruit juice **furu-tsu jyu-su**

fry (verb) **ageru**

frying pan **furai pan**

full (adj) **ippai**; *I'm full* **onaka ga ippai desu**

full board **shokuji tsuki**

funny (adj); **omoshiroi** (odd) **okashih**

furnished (adj): *is it furnished?* **kagu tsuki desuka**

furniture **kagu**

futon **futon**

G

game controller **gehmu kontorohrah**

garage (parking) **shako**; (petrol)

gasorin sutando; (repairs) **kuruma shu-ri ya**

garden **niwa**

gardener **niwashi**

garlic **ninniku**

gate **gehto, mon**; (boarding at airport) **tohjyoh guchi**

gay (adj) (happy) **yohki (na)**; (homosexual) **homosekusharu**

gear **giya**

gearbox **gia bokkusu**

gear lever **giya rebah**

geisha (girl) **geisha**

get (verb) (fetch) **motte kuru**; *have you got...?* **...o omochi desuka**; *to get the train* **densha ni noru**; *to get back: we get back tomorrow* **ashita kaerimasu**; *to get something back* **kaeshite morau**; *get in* (to car, etc) **noru**; (arrive) **tsuku**; *get out* (of bus, etc) **oriru**; *get up* (rise) **okiru**

general hospital **sohgoh byoh-in**

gift **omiyage, okurimono**; *gift* (to landlord) **reikin**

gigabytes **gigabaito**

gin **jin**

girl **onna no ko**

girlfriend **gahrufurendo**

give (verb) **ageru**

glad (adj) **ureshih**; *I'm glad* **ureshih desu**

glass (for drinking) **gurasu**

glasses **megane**

gloss prints **kohtaku no aru purinto**

gloves **tebukuro**

glue **nori**

go (verb) **iku**; *am/are/is going* **ikimasu**; *am not/aren't/isn't going* **ikimasen**; *where are you going?* **doko iku**; *no*; *I'm going to... ...ni ikimasu**

golf **gorufu**; *golf course* **gorufu kohsu**

golfer **gorufah**

goggles (swimming) **suichu megane**; (ski) **gohguru**

gold **kin**

good (adj) **ih**; *good!* **yokatta**; *good morning* **ohayoh gozaimasu**; *good evening* **konbanwa**; *good for me* **daijyohbu**

goodbye (informal) **sayonara**; (formal) **sayohnara**

government **seifu**

grandchild **mago**

grandfather **ojihsan**; *my grandfather* **sofu**

grandmother **obahsan**; *my grandmother* **sobo**

grapes **budoh**

grass **kusa**

Great Britain **igirisu**

green (adj) **midori, gurihn**

greengrocer **yao ya**

grey (adj) **hai-iro** (**no**)

grill (verb) **guriru**

grilled (adj) **yaita**

grocer (shop)
  shokuryoh hinten

ground floor **ikkai**

guarantee **hoshoh-sho**; (verb)
  hoshoh suru

guest **okyaku**

guesthouse **minshuku**

guide dog **mohdohken**

guidebook **gaido bukku**

guided tour **gaido tsuki tsuah**

guitar **gitah**

gun (rifle) **jyu, raifuru**; (pistol)
  pisutoru

gutter **amadoi**

gym **jimu**

H

hair **kami**; (short in length) **kami
  ga mijikai**; (hair streaked with
  grey) **shiraga majiri**

haircut (for man) **sanpatsu**; (for
  woman) **katto**

hairdresser **biyoh in**

hair dryer **doraiyah**

hair spray **hea supureh**

half **hanbun**; *half an hour*
  sanjippun; *half past one* **ichi
  ji han**

half board **chohshoku to
  yu-shoku tsuki**

ham **hamu**; *ham and eggs*
  hamu-eggu; (sandwich)
  hamusando

hamburger **hanbahgah**

hammer **kanazuchi**

hand **te**

hand luggage **kinai mochikomi
  tenmotsu**

hand sanitizer **hando sanitaizah**

handbag **handobaggu**

hand brake **hando
  burehki**

handkerchief **hankachi**

handle (door) **handoru**

handsome **hansamu** (**na**)

hand towel **oshibori**

hangover **futsuka-yoi**

happen (verb): *when did
  it happen?* **itsu
  okori mashitaka**

happy (adj) **shiawase** (**na**)

harbour **minato**

hard (adj) **katai**;
  (difficult) **muzukashih**

hard drive **hahdo doraibu**

hard disk **hahdo disuku**

hard lenses (contact)
  hahdo renzu

harmony **chohwa,
  hahmonih**

hat **bohshi**

hate (verb): *I hate…* **watashi
  wa…ga daikirai desu**

have (verb) **motsu**; *I have… …ga/
  wa arimasu/imasu, …o motte
  imasu*; *I don't have… …ga/wa
  arimasen/imasen, …o motte
  imasen*; *can I have…?* **…o
  kudasai**; *have you got…?*
  …o omochi desuka; *I have a
  headache* **zutsu ga shimasu**

hay fever **kafunshoh**

he **kare**

head **atama**

headache **zutsu**

headphones **heddofon**

headlights **heddo raito**

head office **honsha**

hear **kiku**

hearing aid **hochohki**

heart **shinzoh**

heart attack **shinzoh mahi**

heat **netsu**

heating **danboh**

heavy (adj) **omoi**

heel **kakato**

hello! **konnichiwa**; (on the
  telephone) **moshi moshi**

help **enjo, tasuke**; (verb) **tasukeru**;
  help! **tasukete**; *help me*
  tetsudatte

hepatitis **kan-en**

her: *it's her* **kanojo desu**; *it's for
  her* **kanojo no desu**; *give it to
  her* **kanojo ni agete kudasai**;
  her book(s) **kanojo no hon**; *it's
  hers* **kanojo no** (**mono**) **desu**

high (adj) **takai**

high-speed train ("bullet")
  shinkansen

hill **oka**

him: *it's him* **kare desu**; *it's for him*
  kare no desu; *give it to him*
  kare ni agete kudasai

hire (verb) **kariru**

his: *his shoe(s)* **kare no kutsu**; *it's
  his* **kare no** (**mono**) **desu**

history **rekishi**

hit: *to hit* (percussion instruments)
  (verb) **tatakimasu**

hitchhike (verb) **hicchi-haiku**

HIV positive **eichi ai bui
  kansensya**

hobby **shumi**

holiday **yasumi**; *public holiday*
  shuku jitsu

home **ie**

homeopathy **dohshu
  ryoh hoh**

honest (adj) **shohjiki** (**na**)

honey **hachimitsu**

honeymoon **shinkon-ryokoh**

horn (car) **kurakushon**

horrible (adj) **osoroshih**

hors d'oeuvres **ohdoburu**

horse **uma**

hospital **byoh-in**; *general* **sohgoh
  byoh-in**; *teaching* **daigaku
  byoh-in**

host/hostess **shusaisha, shohtai
  sha, hosuto**

hot (adj) **atsui**

hot chocolate (cocoa) **kokoa**

hot spring (day trip) **higeri-onsen**

hot water bottle **yutanpo**

hotel **hoteru**

hour **jikan**

house **ie**

household products
  kateh yoh hin

househusband/housewife
  sengyo-shufu

how? **doh**; *how much?* **ikura
  desuka**; **dorekurai**

hundred (adj) **hyaku**; *three
  hundred* (adj) **san-byaku**

hungry (adj): *I'm hungry*
  onaka ga suite imasu

hurry: *I'm in a hurry* **isoide
  imasu**

hurt (verb): *will it hurt?*
  itai desuka

husband **goshujin**;
  my husband **otto**

I

I **watashi**

I would like… **ga hoshih desu**

ice **kohri**

ice cream **aisukurihmu**

ice lolly **aisukyandih**

identification **mibun
  shohmeisho, ID**

if **moshi**

ignition **tenka sohchi**

ill (adj) **byohki**

illness **shinkoku** (**na**)

immediately **suguni**

impossible (adj) **fukanoh** (**na**)

in: *in Japan* **nihon ni**; *in Japanese*
  nihongo de; *in my room*
  watashi no heya ni

India **indo**

Indian (person) **indo jin**;
  (adj) **indo no**

indicator **winkah**

indigestion **shohka-furyoh**

infection **kansen**

information **johhoh**

information desk **madoguchi**

information technology **ai-tih**

inhaler (for asthma, etc)
  kyu-nyu-ki

injection **chu-sha**

injury **kega**

ink **inku**

inn (traditional Japanese) **ryokan**

insect **mushi**

insect repellent **mushi yoke
  supureh**

insomnia **fuminshoh**

insurance **hoken**

intend **tsumori**

interesting (adj) **omoshiroi**

internet **intahnetto**

internet café **netto kafeh**

interpret (verb) **tsu-yaku suru**

invitation **shohtai**
invoice **sehkyu-sho**
Ireland **airurando**
Irish (adj) **Airurando no**
Irishman **airurando jin**
Irishwoman **airurando jin**
iron (metal) **tetsu**; (verb: for clothes) **airon o kakeru**
ironmonger **kanamono ya**
is: he/she/it is... **kare wa/kanojo wa/sore wa... desu**
isn't: isn't coming **ga kimasen**
island **shima**
it **sore**
IT **"ai-tih"**
itch **kayumi**; (verb) *it itches* **kayui desu**

J

jacket **jyaketto**
jacuzzi **jagujih**
jam **jamu**
January **ichi gatsu**
Japan **nihon**
Japanese (person) **nihonjin**; (adj) **nihon no**; (language) **nihongo**
Japanese-style (adj) **wafu**; (cuisine) **nihon shoku/washoku**
jazz **jazu**
jealous (adj) **shitto-bukai**
jeans **jihnzu**
jelly **zerih**; (Japanese) **kanten**
jellyfish **kurage**
jeweller **hohseki shoh**
jewellery store **hohseki ten**
job **shigoto**
jog (verb) **jogingu suru**; *to go for a jog* **jogingu ni iku**
joke **johdan**
journey **ryokoh, tabi**
July **shichi gatsu**
jumper **janpah, sehtah**
June **roku gatsu**
just: it's just arrived **chohdo tsuki-mashita**; *I've just got one left* **hitotsu dake nokotte imasu**

K

karaoke (bar) **karaoke**
keen (adj) **nesshin (na)**
key **kih; kagi**
keyboard **kihbohdo**
kidney **jinzoh**
kilo **kiro**
kilometre **kiromehtoru**
kimono **kimono**
kimono, summer casual **yukata**
kind (what kind of tree is this?) **shurui**
kiss **kisu**
kitchen **daidokoro**; (with dining room) **dainingu kicchin**

knee **hiza**
knife **naifu**
knit (verb) **amu**
know (verb): *I don't know* **shirimasen**
Korea **kankoku**; *North Korea* **kita chohsen**; *South Korea* **daikanminkoku**
Korean (person) **kankoku jin**; (adj) **kankoku no**

L

label **raberu**
lace **rehsu**
lacquerware **nurimono**
lady **fujin, jyoseh**
lake **mizu-umi**
lamb (animal) **kohitsuji**; (meat) **ramu**
lamp **ranpu; denki stando**
lampshade **denki stando no kasa**
land **tochi**; (verb) **chakuriku suru**
landscape (scenery) **keshiki**
language **gengo**
laptop (computer) **nohto pasokon**
large (adj) **ohkih**
last (final) **saigo (no)**; *last week* **senshu**; *last month* **sen getsu**; *at last!* **tsui ni**
late: it's getting late **moh osoi desu**; (adj) *the train is late* **densha wa okurete imasu**
laugh **warai**; (verb) **warau**
launderette **koin-randorih**
laundry (place) **kurihningu ya**; (dirty clothes) **sentaku-mono**
law (field of study) **hohritsu, hohgaku**
lawyer **bengo shi**
laxative **gezai**
lazy (adj): *he is a lazy person* **kare wa namake-mono desu**
lead (pets) **rihdo**
leaf **ha, happa**
leaflet **chirashi**
learn (verb) **narau, manabu**
leather **kawa**
leave (verb): *go away* **deru, saru**; (object) **nokosu**
lecture **kohgi**;*lecture theatre* **kohdoh**; *lecture* (university) **kohgi**
lecturer **kohshi**
left (not right) **hidari**; *turn left* **hidari ni magatte kudasai**
left luggage **tenimotsu azukarisho**; (locker) **rokkah**
leg **ashi**
leisure **rejyah**
lemon **remon**
lemonade **remonehdo**
length **nagasa**
lens **renzu**
less: less than... **...yori sukunai**
lesson **jugyoh**
letter **tegami**

letterbox **yu-bimbako**
lettuce **retasu**
library **toshokan**
licence **menkyo**
lie down **yoko ni naru**
life **seikatsu**
lift (in building) **erebehtah**; *could you give me a lift?* **nosete kure-masenka**
light (adj) (not heavy) **karui**; (not dark) **akarui**
lighter **raitah**
lighter fuel **raitah no gasu**
light meter **roshutsukei**
like (verb): *I like...* **...ga suki desu**; *I don't like it* **suki dewa arimasen**; *I'd like...* **...o onegai shimasu, ...o kudasai**
lime (fruit) **raimu**
line (underground, etc) **sen**
lip salve **rippu-kurihmu**
lipstick **kuchi-beni**
liqueur **rikyu-ru**
list **risuto**
literature (field of study) **bungaku**
litre **rittoru**
litter **gomikuzu**
little (adj, small) **chihsai**; *just a little* **hon no sukoshi**
liver (organ) **kanzoh**; (food) **rebah**
living room **ima, ribingu**
lobster **ise-ebi**
local train **futsu (ressha)**
lollipop **boh tsuki kyandeh**
long (adj) **nagai**; *long hair* **kami ga nagai**; *how long does it take?* **dono kurai kakari masuka**
lorry **torakku**
lost **michi ni mayotta**
lost property **wasure-mono**
lot: a lot **takusan**; *not a lot* **ohku arimasen**
loud (adj): *in a loud voice* **ohgoe de**
lounge **raunji**
love **ai**; (verb) **ai suru**
love hotels **rabuhoteru**
lover **koibito**
low (adj) **hikui**
low dining table **chabudai**
luck **un**; *good luck!* **guddo rakku, ganbatte**
luggage **tenimotsu**
luggage rack **nimotsu-dana**
lunch **chu-shoku**; (boxed lunch) **bento**

M

magazine **zasshi**
mail (verb) **yu-soh suru yu-bin-butsu**
main courses **mein kohsu**
make (verb) **tsukuru**
make-up **keshoh hin**
man **otoko, danseh, hito**

manager **manehjyah**; (level of seniority) *MD* **shacho**; *division* **senmu**; *department* **bucho**; *section* **kacho**; *team* **kakaricho**

map **chizu**; *a map of Tokyo* **Tohkyoh no chizu**; (online map) **onrain chizu**

March **san gatsu**

margarine **mahgarin**

market **ichiba**

marmalade **mahmarehdo**

married (adj): *I'm married* **kekkon shite imasu**

martial arts **budoh**

mascara **masukara**

massage **massahji**

master's **shuhshi**

mat (straw) **tatami**

match (light) **macchi**; (sport) **shiai**

material (cloth) **kiji**

matter: what's the matter? **doh shimashitaka**

mattress **mattoresu; shikibuton**

May **go gatsu**

may be **tabun**

mayonnaise **mayonehzu**

me: it's me **watashi desu**; *it's for me* **watashi no desu**; *give it to me* **watashi ni kudasai**

meal **shokuji**

meat **niku**; *meatball* **nikudango**

mechanic **kikai gishi**

medicine (tablets, etc) **kusuri**; (field of study) **igaku**

meet **au**; *Pleased to meet you* **dohzo yoroshiku**

meeting **mihtingu, kaigi**

melon **meron**

memory (computer) **memori**

men (toilet) **dansei yoh toire**

menu **menyu**

message **messehji**

metro **metoro, chikatetsu**; *metro station* **chikatetsu no eki**

microwave **denshi renji**

midday **shohgo**

middle: in the middle **mannaka ni**

midnight **mayonaka**

milk **gyu-nyu, miruku**

million (adj) **hyaku-man**

mine: it's mine **watashi no (mono) desu**

mineral water **mineraru wohtah**

minestrone **minestorohne**

minibar **minibah**

minimum speed limit **saiteh sokudo**

minute **fun**

mirror **kagami**

mist (onsen) **yu kemuri**

mistake **machigai**; *I made a mistake* **machigai-mashita**

mobile phone **kehtai (denwa)**

modem **modem**

monastery **shu-dohin**

Monday **getsuyohbi**

money **okane**

monkey **saru**

monitor **monitah**

month **tsuki, ...gatsu**

monument **kinenhi**

moon **tsuki**

moped **tansha**

more **motto**

morning **asa**; *good morning* **ohayoh gozaimasu**; *in the morning* **asa ni**

mosaic **mozaiku**

mosquito **ka**

mother **okahsan**; *my mother* **haha** *my mother-in-law* **giri no haha**

motorbike **ohtobai**

motorboat **mohtah-bohto**

motorway **kohsoku dohro**

Mount Fuji **fujisan**

mountain **yama**; *mountain climbing* **tozan**

mouse (animal) **nezumi**; (computer) **mausu**

moustache **kuchi hige**

mouth **kuchi**

move (verb) **ugoku**; *don't move!* **ugokanaide**; (house) **hikkosu**; *When can I move in?* **itsu nyu-kyo dekimasuka**

movie **eiga**

Mr, Mrs, Ms **-san**

much: not much **sukoshi**; *much better* **zutto, ih desu**

mug **kappu**

mum **okahsan**

museum **hakubutsukan**

mushroom **kinoko, masshurumu**

music **ongaku**

musical instrument **gakki**

musician **ongakuka**

mussels **mu-rugai**

mustard **karashi**

my: my key(s) **watashi no kagi**

mythology **shinwa**

N

nail (metal) **kugi**; (finger) **tsume**

nail file **nehru-fairu**

nail polish **manikyua**

name **namae**; *my name is...* **watashi no namae wa... desu**

nappies **omutsu**; *disposable nappies* **kami omutsu**

narrow **semai**

National Police Agency **keisatsu choh**

near: near the door **doa no chikaku**; *near London* **rondon no chikaku**

necessary **hitsuyoh**

neck **kubi**

necklace **nekkuresu**

need (verb) **iru**; *I need...* **watashi wa... ga irimasu**; *... are needed* **...ga hitsuyoh desu**

needle **hari**

negative (photo) **nega**

neither: neither of them **dochira mo... masen**; *neither... nor... mo... mo... masen*

nephew **oi**

never **kesshite**

new **atarashih**

New Year **oshogatsu**; *New Year's eve* **ohmisoka**

news **nyu-su**

newsagent **shinbun ya**

newspaper **shinbun**

New Zealand **Nyu-jihrando**

New Zealander (person) **nyu-jihrando jin**

next **tsugi**; *next week* **raishu**; *next month* **rai getsu**

nice **suteki (na)**; *how nice!* **ih desune**

niece **mei**

night **yoru**; *two nights* (stay in hotel) **ni haku**; *three nights* (stay in hotel) **san paku**

nightclub **naito-kurabu**

nightdress **nemaki**

nine (adj, numeral) **kyu**; *nine people* (classifier) **kyu nin**

nineteen (adj) **jyu-kyu**

ninety (adj) **kyu-jyu**

no (response) **ihe**; *I have no money* **okane wa arimasen**; *no entry* **shin-nyu kinshi**; *no problem* **ihdesuyo**

noisy (adj) **urusai, yakamashih**

non-smoking (adj) (section) **kin-en seki**

noodles **men rui**; (Chinese) **ramen**; (Chinese, fried) **yakisoba**

normal **futsu**

north **kita**

Northern Ireland **kita airurando**

nose **hana**

not: not today **kyoh dewa arimasen**; *he is not here* **kare wa koko ni imasen**; *not that one* **sore dewa arimasen**

not come **kimasen**; *not coming* **kimasen**

notepad **nohto**

notes (money) **shiheh**

nothing **nanimo**

novel **shohsetsu**

November **jyu-ichi gatsu**

now **ima**

nowhere **dokonimo**

number (numeral) **su-ji**; (telephone) **bangoh**

number plate **nambah-purehto**

nurse **kangoshi**

nut **nattsu**;(fruit) **kurumi**; (for bolt) **natto**

O

occasionally **tama ni**

o'clock: ... o'clock **...ji**

October **jyu gatsu**

octopus **tako**
of **...no** *the name of the street* **michi no namae**
off-licence **saka ya**
office **jimusho**; *office block* **ofisu biru**; *office worker* **kaisha in**
often **yoku, tabi tabi**
oil **oiru, sekiyu, abura**
ointment **nankoh**
OK **okkeh**
old (adj) (thing) **furui**; (person) **toshi o totta**
olive **orihbu**
omelette **omuretsu**; (Japanese) **tamago-yaki**
on **ue**; *on the table* **tehburu no ue ni**
one (adj, numeral) **ichi**; (+ noun) **hitotsu** (**no**); *one person* (classifier) **hitori**; *one million* (adj) **hyaku-man**; *one o'clock* **ichi ji**
one way **ippoh tsu-koh**
onion **tamanegi**
online maps **onrain chizu**
only **...dake**
open (adj) **aita**; (verb) **akeru**; *what time do you open?* **nanji ni akimasuka**
opening times (museums/ libraries) **kaikan jiman**; (shops/restaurants) **eigyoh jikan**
operating theatre **shujyutsu shitsu**
opposite (adj) **hantai gawa**; *opposite the hotel* **hoteru no hantai gawa**
or **soretomo, aruiwa**
orange (adj) (colour) **orenji-iro** (**no**); (fruit) **orenji**
orange juice **orenj jyusu**
orchestra **ohkesutora**
order **chu-mon; ohdah**
ordinary (adj) **futsu-no**
our **watashi tachi no**; *it's ours* **watashi tachi no** (**mono**) **desu**
out (adj): *he's out* **kare wa gaishutsu shite imasu**
outside **soto**
over (more than) **ijyoh**; (above) **ue**; *over there* **mukoh**
overtake (verb) **oikosu**
oyster **kaki**

P

Pacific Ocean **taiheiyoh**
package (parcel) **kozutsumi**
packet **pakku**; *a packet of...* **...hitohako**
pack of cards **kahdo hitokumi**
padlock **nankinjoh**
pagoda **toh**; (five-storeyed) **gojyu no toh**; (three-storeyed) **sanjyu no toh**
page **pehji**

pain **itai; itami**
paint **penki**
painting (hobby) **e o kaku koto**
pair **futatsu** (**no**), **ittsui** (**no**); *a pair of shoes* **kutsu issoku**
Pakistan **pakisutan**
Pakistani (person) **pakisutan jin**; (adj) **pakisutan no**
pale (adj) (face) **kaoiro ga warui**; (colour) **usui**
pancakes **pankehki**
paper **kami**; (newspaper) **shinbun**
paper lantern **chochin**
parcel **kozutsumi**
pardon? **e? nan desuka**
parents **ryohshin**
park **kohen**; (verb) **chu-sha suru**
parking: no parking **chus-sha kinshi**; *parking garage* **shako**
party (celebration) **pahtih**; (group) **dantai**; (political) **seitoh**
passenger **ryokyaku**
passport **pasupohto**; *passport control* (entering) **nyu-koku shinsa**; (leaving) **shukkoku shinsa**
password **pasuwahdo**; *Wi-Fi password* **wai fai pasuwahdo**
path **komichi**
patient (in hospital) **kanja, byoh-nin**
pavement **hodoh**
pay (verb) **harau** *where can I pay?* **doko de harae masuka**
payment **shiharai**
peach **momo, pihchi**
peaceful **nodoka**
peanuts **pihnatsu**
pear **nashi**
pearl **shinju, pahru**
peas **mame**
pedestrian **hokohsha**
peg (clothes) **sentaku-basami**
pen **pen**
penicillin **penishirin**
pencil **enpitsu**
pencil sharpener **enpitsu kezuri**
penfriend **penparu**
peninsula **hantoh**
penknife **pen naifu**
penmanship **shu-ji**
people **hitobito** (nation) **kokumin**
pepper (condiment) **koshoh**; (vegetable) **pihman**
peppermints **hakka-dorop, minto**
per **...ni tsuki**; *per person* **hitori ni tsuki**
perfect (adj) **kanzen** (**na**)
perfume **kohsui**
perm **pahma**
petrol **gasorin**
petrol station **gasorin sutando**
petticoat **pechikohto**
pharmacy **yakkyoku, kusuriya**
PhD **hakushi**
phonecard **tereka, terehon cahdo**
photocopier **kopihki**
photocopy **kopih**

photograph **shashin**; (verb) **shashin o toru**
photographer **shashinka**
phrase book **furehzubukku**
physics (field of study) **butsuri**
piano **piano**
pickle **tsukemono**
pickpocket **suri**; *I've been pickpocketed* **surare mashita**
picnic **pikunikku**
piece **hitokire, hitotsu**
pig **buta**
pillow **makura**
pilot **pairotto**
pin **pin, anshoh bangoh**
pine (tree) **matsu**
pineapple **painappuru**
pink **pinku** (adj) **pinku no**
pipe (for smoking) **paipu**; (for water) **suidohkan**
pizza **piza**
place **basho**
plants **shokubutsu**
plaster (for cut) **bansohkoh**
plastic **purasuchikku**
plastic bag **binihru-bukuro**
plate **osara**
platform **purrattohohmu**
play: to play (musical instruments); (verb) **hikimasu**
play (theatre) **geki, shibai**
pleasant (adj) **kimochi no ih**
please (give me) (**o**) **onegai shimasu**; (please do) **dohzo**; (formal) **itadake masuka**; *please wait for me* **chotto matte kudasai**
plug (electrical) **konsento, puragu, henkan puragu**; (sink) **sen**
plumber **haikankoh**
pocket **poketto**
poison **doku**
police **kehsatsu**
police officer **kehsatsu kan, omawarisan**
police report **tsuh-hoh**
police station **kehsatsu sho**
politics **seiji**
pond **ike**
poor (adj) **mazushih**; (bad quality) **shitsu ga warui**
pop music **poppu**
porch **engawa, pohchi**
pork **butaniku, pohku**
port (harbour) **minato**
porter **pohtah**
possible (adj) **kanoh** (**na**)
post **posuto**; (verb) **posuto ni ireru**
postbox **posuto**
postcard **hagaki**
poster **posutah**
postman **yu-bin haitatsu nin**
post office **yu-bin kyoku**
potato **poteto, jyagaimo**; *potato salad* **poteto sarada**

poultry **toriniku**; (dishes) **tori-ryohri**

pound (money) **pondo**

powder **kona, paudah**

pram **uba-guruma**

prawn **ebi**; *king prawn* **kuruma ebi**

prefer **...ga suki**

pregnant (adj): *I'm pregnant* **ninshin shite imasu**

preparation **jyunbi**

prescription **shohohsen**

pretty (beautiful) (adj) **kirei (na)**

price **nedan**

priest (Shintoh) **kannushi**; (Buddhist) **obohsan**; (Christian) **bokushi**

printer **purintah**

private (adj) **kojin (no)**

problem **mondai**; *what's the problem?* **doh shimashitaka**

proceed slowly **jyokoh**

profession: what's your profession? **goshokugyoh wa**

professor **kyohjyu**

profits **ri-eki**

progress **shinpo**

pub (informal) **izakaya**

public **ohyake**

pull (verb) **hiku**

puncture **panku**; (verb) **panku suru**

purple **murasaki**; (adj) **murasaki no**

purse **saifu**

push (verb) **osu**

pushchair **uba-guruma**

put (verb) **oku**

pyjamas (traditional Japanese) **pajama**

Q

quality **shitsu**

quay **hatoba**

quarter: past one **ichi ji jyu-go fun**; *to two* ("one forty-five") **ichi ji yonjyu-go fun**

question **shitsumon**

queue **retsu**; (verb) **narabu**

quick (adj) **hayai**

quiet (adj) **shizuka (na)**

quite (adj) (fairly) **kanari**; (fully) **sukkari**

R

rabbit **usagi**

radiator **rajiehtah**

radio **rajio**

radish **daikon**; (pickled, yellow) **takuan**

railway **tetsudoh**

rain **ame**

raincoat **reinkohto**

raisins **hoshi-budoh, rehzun**

rapid train **kaisoku**

rare (adj) (uncommon) **mezurashih**; (steak) **re-ah**

rash **kabure, hosshin**

rat **dobu-nezumi**

raw (adj) **nama (no)**

razor blades **kamisori no ha**

read (verb) **yomu**

reading **dokusho**; *reading lamp* **dokusho ranpu**

ready (adj) (I'm ready) **yohi ga deki-mashita**; *ready meals* **chorizumi shokuhin**

rear lights **tehru-ranpu**

receipt **reshihto, ryohshu-sho**

reception **uketsuke; kangeikai**; (party) **resepushion**

recommend **susumeru**

record (music) **rekohdo**; (sporting, etc) **kiroku**

record player **rekohdo-purehyah**

red **aka**; (adj) **akai**

registered post **kakitome yu-bin**

relatives (family) **shinseki**

relax (verb) **yukkuri suru**

religion **shu-kyoh**

remember (verb) **oboete iru**; *I don't remember* **oboete imasen**

rent **yachin**; (verb) **kasu**

repairs **shu-ri**; *repairperson* **shu-ri koh**

repeat **kurikaeshi**; (verb) **kurikaesu**

report **hohkoku sho, repohto**

requests (please do...) **shite kudasai**

research **kenkyu**

reservation **yoyaku**

rest (remainder) **sono hoka**; (relaxation) (verb) **yasumu**

restaurant **resutoran**; *high-end restaurant* **ryohtei**

return (verb) (come back) **kaeru**; (give back) **kaesu**

return (ticket) **ohfuku**

review **fukushu**

rice (uncooked) **kome**; (cooked) **gohan**; (dishes) **gohan-mono**; (fried) **chah-han**; (with chicken) **chikin raisu**

rice cooker **suihanki**

rice cake **omochi/mochi**

rich (adj) (person) **kanemochi (no)**; (food) **kotteri shita**

right (adj) (correct) **tadashih**; *that's right* **sohdesu**; (direction) **migi**; *turn right* **migi ni magatte kudasai**

ring (verb) (to call) **denwa suru**; (wedding, etc) **yubiwa**

ripe (adj) **jukushita**

river **kawa**

road **dohro, michi**

roasted (adj) **rohsuto shita**

robe, summer casual (kimono) **yukata**

rock (stone) **ishi** (music) **rokku**

roll (bread) **rohru-pan**

roof **yane**

room **heya**; (space) **basho, supehsu**

rope **tsuna, rohpu**

rose **bara**

round (adj) (circular) **marui**; *it's my round* **watashi no ban desu**

route (bus, etc) **sen**

rowing boat **bohto**

rubber (eraser) **keshigomu**; (material) **gomu**

rubbish (refuse) **gomi** (poor quality) **garakuta**

ruby (stone) **rubih**

rucksack **ryukku sakku**

rug (mat) **shikimono**; (blanket) **mohfu**

ruins **haikyo, iseki**

ruler (for drawing) **johgi**

rum **ramu**

run (verb) (person) **hashiru**

Russia **Roshia**

Russian (person) **roshia jin**; (adj) **roshia no**

S

sad (adj) **kanashih**

safe (adj) **anzen (na)**

safety pin **anzen-pin**

sailing boat **hansen**

saki **osake**

salad **sarada**

salami **sarami**

salary man **sararihman**

sale (at reduced prices) **sehru**

sales (figures) **uri age**

salmon **sake**

salt **shio**

same (adj): *the same dress* **onaji doresu**; *the same people* **onaji hito**; *same again please* **onajino o moh hitotsu, onegai shimasu**

sand **suna**

sandals **sandaru**

sand dunes **sakyu**

sandwich **sando icchi**

sanitary towels **seiriyoh napkin**

sash **obi**

satellite TV **sateraito terebi, ehseh terebi**

Saturday **doyohbi**

sauce **sohsu**

saucepan **nabe**

sauna **sauna**

sausage **sohsehji**

sax **sakkusu**

say (verb) **yu**; *what did you say?* **nan to iware mashitaka**; *how do you say... in Japanese?* **...wa nihongo de nanto ihmasuka**

scarf **sukahfu**
school **gakkoh**
schedule **sukejyu-ru**
science (field of study) **kagaku**
scissors **hasami**
Scotland **Sukottorando**
Scottish (adj) **sukottorando no**
screen (computer, etc) **gamen**
screen door (ryokan) **fusuma**
screw **neji**
screwdriver **neji-mawashi,
    sukuryu doraibah**
scroll **makimono**
sea **umi**
seafood **shihfu-do**
seal (official) **inkan**
season **kisetsu**
seat **seki**
seat belt **shihto-beruto**
second (adj) **nibanme (no)**;
    (time) **byoh**
secretary **hisho**
see (verb) **miru**; *I can't see*
    miemasen; *I see* (understand)
    soh desuka, wakarimashita
self-employed **ji-eigyoh**
sell (verb) **uru**
seminar **zemi, seminah**
send (verb) **okuru**
separate (adj) **betsu (no)**;
    separately **betsubetsu**
separated (adj) (from husband,
    etc) **wakareta**
September **ku gatsu**
serious (adj) (situation) **jyu-dai
    (na)** (person) **majime (na)**
server (waiter/waitress) **uehtah/
    uehtoresu**
service **sahbisu**
serviette **napukin**
set (in theatre) **setto**
set menus **teishoku**
seven (adj, numeral) **shichi,
    nana**; *seven people* (classifier)
    shichi nin
seventeen (adj) **jyu-shichi,
    jyu-nana**
seventy (adj) **nana-jyu**
several (adj) **ikutsuka (no)**
sew (verb) **nuu**
shampoo **shanpu**
shave **hige-sori**; (verb) **hige o soru**
shaving foam **shehbingu fohmu**
shawl **shohru**
she **kanojo**
sheep **hitsuji**
sheet **shihtsu**
shell **kai, kaigara**
sherry **sherih**
Shinto (adj) **shintoh no**
Shintoism **shintoh**
ship **fune**
shirt **shatsu**
shoelaces **kutsu-himo**
shoe polish **kutsu-zumi**
shoe shop **kutsu ya**
shoe size **kutsu no saizu**
shoes **kutsu**

shop **mise**
shopkeeper **tenshu**
shopping (verb) **kaimono,
    shoppingu**; *to go shopping*
    kaimono ni iku; *shopping trolley*
    shoppingu kahto; *shopping
    mall* **shoppingu mohru**;
    shopping arcade **shotengei**
short (adj) (object) **mijikai**;
    (person) **(se ga) hikui**;
    (hair) **kami ga mijikai**
shorts **hanzubon, shohtsu**
shoulder **kata**
show **shoh**
shower (bath) **shawah**; (rain)
    niwaka ame
shower gel **shawah jeru**
shrimp **ebi**
shrine **jinja**
shutter (window) **amado**;
    (camera) **shattah**
siblings **go kyohdai**; *my
    siblings* **kyohdai**
sick (adj) (ill) **byohki**; *I feel sick*
    kimochi ga warui desu
side (edge) **hashi**; *I'm on her
    side* **watashi wa kanojo
    no mikata desu**
sidelights **saido-raito**
sights: the sights of... **...no
    kenbutsu**
sightseeing (verb) **kankoh**
sign (verb) **shomei suru**
signature **sain**
silk **kinu**
silver (adj) (colour) **giniro (no)**;
    (metal) **gin**
simmered **nita**; (food) **nimono**
simple (adj) **kantan (na),
    shinpuru (na)**
SIM card **simu cahdo**
sing (verb) **utau**
single (adj) (one) **hitotsu**;
    (unmarried) **dokushin**
single room **shinguru ru-mu**
single (adj) (ticket) **katamichi**
sink (kitchen) **nagashi**
sister (older) **ane**; (younger)
    imohto
sit (verb) **suwaru**
six (adj, numeral) **roku**; *six
    people* (classifier) **roku
    nin**; *six lakh* **rokujyu-man
    nin**
sixteen (adj) **jyu-roku**
sixty (adj) **roku-jyu**
size (clothes) **saizu**
skid (verb) **suberu**
skiing **sukih**
skin cleanser **kurenjingu-
    kurihm**
skirt **sukahto**
sky **sora**
sleep **suimin**; (verb) **nemuru**;
    to go to sleep **neru**
sleeping bag **nebukuro**
sleeping pill **suimin-yaku**
sleeve **sode**

sliding door **hikido**
sliding paper door/window
    (ryokan) **shoji**
slippers **surippa**
slow (adj) **osoi**
small (adj) **chihsai**
smell **nioi** (verb) **niou**
smile **hohoemi**; (verb) **hohoemu**
smoke **kemuri**; (verb) **tabako o su**
smoking (section) **kitsu-en seki**
snacks (confectionery) **okashi**;
    (confectionery category) **kashi
    rui**; *(crisp, popcorn, etc)*
    sunakku; *(afternoon snack)*
    oyatsu; *(light meal)* **keishoku**
snow **yuki**
snow-view (onsen) **yukimi onsen**
so: so good **totemo ih**; *not so
    much... * **sore hodo... dewa
    arimasen**
soaking solution (for contact
    lenses) **kontakutoyoh
    hozon eki**
soap **sekken**
socks **kutsushita**
soda water **sohdasui**
sofa **sofah**
soft (adj) **yawarakai**
soft lenses **softo-renzu**
soil (earth) **tsuchi**
somebody **dareka**
somehow **nantoka, dohnika**
something **nanika**
sometimes **tokidoki**
somewhere **dokoka**
son **musuko san**; *my son* **musuko**
song **uta**
soon **moh sugu**; *see you
    soon* **dewa mata**
sorbet **shahbetto**
sorry! **gomennasai**
    I'm sorry **sumimasen**
soup **supu**; (dishes) **shirumono**
south **minami**
South Africa **Minami Afurika**
South African (person) **minami
    afurika jin**; (adj) **minami
    afurika no**
soufflé **sufere**
souvenir **omiyage**
souvenir shop **miyabe ya**
soy sauce **shoyu**
soyabean **daizu**
soyabean (fermented) **nattoh**;
    (fermented paste) **miso**
spas with hot springs **onsen**
spade (shovel) **suki**;
    (cards) **supehdo**
spaghetti **spagetti**
spanner **spana**
spares **yobi-hin**
spark plug **tenka-puragu**
speak (verb) **hanasu**; *do you
    speak...?* **...o hanashi-masuka**;
    I don't speak... **...wa
    hanashimasen**
spectacles **megane**
speed **supihdo**

speed limit **saikoh sokudo**

spider **kumo**

sponge cake **kasutera**

spoon **supuun**

sport **supohtsu**

sprain **nenza**; (verb) **nenza suru**

spring (season) **haru**; (mechanical) **bane**

square (in town) **hiroba**

stadium **stajiamu**

staff **sutaffu**

stage (in theatre) **butai**

staircase **kaidan**

stairs **kaidan**

stamp (official) **inkan**

stamps **kitte**

stapler **hochikisu**

star **hoshi** (film) **sutah**

start **shuppatsu, sutahto**; (verb) **shuppatsu suru**

starters **zen sai**

statement (to police) **hohkoku sho**

station **eki**

statue **dohzoh**

steamed (adj) (food) **mushita**; (dishes) **mushimono**

steal (verb) **nusumu**; *it's been stolen* **nusumare-mashita**

steps **kaidan**

sticky tape **serotehpu**

stockings **sutokkingu**

stomach **onaka**

stomach ache **fukutsu**

stop (verb) **tomaru**; (bus stop) **basutei**; *stop!* **tomare**

storm **arashi**

stove (kitchen) **renji, konro**

straight on **massugu ni**

strawberry **ichigo, sutoroberih**

stream **ogawa**

street **michi; dohro**; *first street on the left* **hidari gawa no saisho no michi**; *second street on the right* **migi no ni-banme no michi**; *at the end of the street* **michi no owari ni**

street stall **yatai**

string (cord) **himo, kohdo**; (guitar, etc) **gen**

student **gakusei**

stupid (adj) **baka**

suburbs **kohgai**

sugar **satoh**

suit **su-tsu** (verb) **au, niau**; *it suits you* **anata ni niaimasu**

suitcase **su-tsu kehsu**

summer **natsu**

sumo (verb) **sumoh**

sun **taiyoh**

sunbathe **nikkohyoku**

sunburn **hiyake**

Sunday **nichiyohbi**

sunglasses **sangurasu**

sunny (adj): *it's sunny* **hi ga dete imasu, tenki ga ih desu**

suntan **hiyake**

suntan lotion **hiyake rohshon**

supermarket **su-pah**

supplement (for fares) **tsuika ryohkin**

suppository **zayaku**

surname **myohji**

sushi **osushi**

sweat **ase**; (verb) **ase o kaku**

sweatshirt **torehnah**

sweet (adj) (not sour) **amai**; (candy) **kyandih**

sweet cafés (Japanese) **amamidokoro**

swimming **suiei**; *swimming costume* **mizuigi**; *swimming pool* **suimingu pu-ru**

switch **suicchi**

syringe **chu-sha ki**

syrup **shiroppu**

T

table **tehburu**

tablet **jyohzai**

Taiwan **Taiwan**

take (verb) **noru**; *I want to take the train* **densha ni noritai desu**; *can I take it with me?* **motte itte mo ih desuka**; *we'll take it* **kore ni shimasu**

take away (verb) **mochi-kaeri**

takeoff (verb) **ririku**

talcum powder **tarukamu-paudah**

talk **hanashi**; (verb) **hanasu**

tall (adj) **takai**

tampon **tanpon**

tangerine **mikan**

tank **tanku**

tap **jyaguchi**

tapestry **tapesutorih**

tax: *including tax* **zeikomi**

taxi **takushih**

taxi rank **takushih noriba**

tea **cha, tih**; (Japanese) **ocha**; (types of ocha) **sencha, ryokucha**; (Western, black, literally "red tea") **kohcha**; (with milk) **miruku tih**

teacup **yunomi**

teach (verb) **oshieru**

teacher **sensei**

teaching hospital **daigaku byoh-in**

teahouse **chaya, chamise**

team **chihmu**

tea towel **fukin**

telephone **denwa**; (verb) **denwa suru, denwa o kakeru**

telephone box **denwa bokkusu**

telephone call **denwa**

telephone number **denwa bangoh**

television **terebi**

temperature **ondo**; (fever) **netsu**

temple **tera**

ten (adj, numeral) **jyu**; *ten people* (classifier) **jyu nin**; *ten minutes* **jippun**; *ten to two* **ni ji jippun mae**

ten thousand (adj) **man, ichi-man**

tennis **tenisu**

tent **tento**

terabytes **terabaito**

terminal (airport) **tahminaru**

than **yori**

thank (verb) **kansha suru**; *thank you* **arigatoh**; *thank you very much* **arigatoh gozaimasu**; *thank you for your call* **odenwa arigatoh gozaimasu**

that: that bus **ano basu**; *what's that?* **a-re wa nan desuka**; *I think that...* **...to omoimasu**

theatre **gekijyoh**

their: their room(s) **karera no heya**; *it's theirs* **karera no (mono) desu**

them: it's them **karera desu**; *it's for them* **karera no desu**; *give it to them* **karera ni agenasai**

theme park **tehma pahku**

then **sore kara, soshite**

there (near you) **soko**; (over there) **asoko**; *there is/are...* **...ga/wa arimasu/imasu**; *there isn't/ aren't...* **...ga/wa arimasen/ imasen**; *is there...?* **...ga/wa arimasuka/imasuka**

these: these things **korera no mono/kore**; *these are mine* **korera wa watashi no (mono) desu**

test (medical) **kensa**

they **karera**

thick (adj) **atsui**

thief **doroboh**

thin (adj) **usui**; (person) **yaseta**

thing (abstract) **koto**; (concrete) **mono**

think (verb) **omou, kangaeru**; *I think so* **soh omoimasu**; *I'll think about it* **kangaete mimasu**

third (adj) **sanbanme**

thirsty (adj): *I'm thirsty* **nodo ga kawaite imasu**

thirteen (adj) **jyu-san**

thirty (adj) **san-jyu**

this: this bus **kono basu**; *what's this?* **kore wa nan desuka**; *this is Mr...* **kochira wa... -san desu**

those: those things **sorera no mono/sore**; *those are his* **sorera wa kare no (mono) desu**

thousand (adj) **sen**; *ten thousand* (adj) **(ichi) man**

three (adj, numeral) **san**; *three people* (classifier) **san nin**

three hundred (adj) **san-byaku**
throat **nodo**
throat pastilles **nodo gusuri, nodo ame**
through: through Tokyo **Tohkyoh keiyu**
thunderstorm **raiu**
Thursday **mokuyohbi**
ticket **chiketto**
tie **nekutai**; (verb) **musubu**
tights **sutokkingu; taitsu**
time **jikan**; *what's the time?* **ima nanji desuka**; *to be on time* **yotei dohri**
timetable **jikoku-hyoh**
tin (can) **kan**
tin opener **kankiri**
tip (money) **chippu**; (end) **saki**
tired (adj) **tsukareta**; *I feel tired* **tsukare-mashita**
tissues **tisshu**
to: to England **igirisu e**; *to the station* **eki e**
toast **tohsuto**
tobacco **tabako**
today **kyoh**
toe **tsumasaki**
tofu **tohfu**; (fried) **abura-age**
tofu shop **tofu ya**
together **issho ni**
toilet **toire**
toilet paper **toiretto pehpah**
Tokyo Metropolitan Police Department **keishi choh**
tomato **tomato**
tomato juice **tomato jyusu**
tomorrow **ashita**; *see you tomorrow* **dewa mata ashita**
tongue **shita**
tonic **tonikku**
tonight **konya**
too (also) **mo**; (excessive) **-sugiru**
took **norimashita**; *take, am/are/is taking* **norimasu**; *don't take, am not/aren't/isn't taking* **norimasen**; *didn't take* **norimasen deshita**
tooth **ha**
toothache **ha-ita**
toothbrush **haburashi**
toothpaste **hamigaki**
torch **kaichu dentoh**
tour **tsuah**; *food tour* (walking) **tabe-aruki**
tourist **ryokoh-sha**
tourist office **kankoh an-naijyo**
tourist spots **kanko-chi**
towel **taoru**
tower **tawah, toh**
town **machi**
town hall **shiyakusho**
toy **omocha**
track suit **undoh-gi**
tractor **torakutah**

trade fair **mihonichi, tenjikai**
tradition **dentoh**
traffic **kohtsuu**
traffic jam **kohtsuu-jyu-tai**
traffic lights **shingoh**
trailer (for car) **torehrah**
train **densha**; *train* (local) **futsu**; *train* (rapid) **kaisoku**; *train* (express) **kyuko, tokkyu**; *train* (high-speed "bullet") **shinkansen**
transformer **hen-atsuki**
translate (verb) **honyaku suru**
transmission (for car) **toransumisshon**
travel agent **ryokoh dairi ten**
travel guide **gaido bukku**
tray **obon, toreh**
travelling (verb) **ryokoh**
tree **ki**
trolley **kahto**
trousers **pantsu; zubon**
try (verb) **yatte miru, tamesu**
Tuesday **kayohbi**
tunnel **tonneru**
tweezers **pinsetto**
twelve (adj) **jyu-ni**
twenty (adj) **ni-jyu**
twenty five (adj) **ni-jyu go**
twenty past one **ichi ji nijippun**
twin room **tsuin ru-mu**
two (adj, numeral) **ni**; *two people* (classifier) **futari**; *two o'clock* **ni ji**
two hundred thousand **ni-jyu-man**
type **taipu**; *what type of... do you have?* **donna taipu no... desuka**
tyre **taiya**

U

ugly (adj) **minikui**
umbrella **kasa**
uncle **ojisan**; *my uncle* **oji**
under (adj) **shita**
underground **chikatetsu**
underground station **chikatetsu no eki**
underwear **shitagi**
unfortunately **zannen nagara**
university **daigaku**; *university lecture* **kohgi**
until... **...ma-de**
unusual (adj) **mezurashii**
up **ue** (upwards) **ue ma-de**
urgent (adj) **kyu (na), isogi no**; *it's urgent* **kinkyu desu**
us: it's us **watashi tachi desu**; *it's for us* **watashi tachi no desu**; *give it to us* **watashi tachi ni kudasai**
USB flash drive **USB furasshu doraibu**
use **shiyoh**; (verb) **tsukau**; *it's no use* **yakuni tachimasen, tsukae masen**

useful (adj) **yakuni tatsu, benri na**
usual (adj) **itsumo no**
usually **itsumo**

V

vacancy (room) **akibeya**
vaccination **yoboh sesshu**
vacuum cleaner **sohjiki**
vacuum flask **mahohbin**
valley **tani**
valve **ben**
vanilla **banira**
vanity box (ryokan) **kyodai**
vase **kabin**
veal **koushi no niku**
vegetables **yasai**
vegetarian (adj) **bejitarian**
vehicle **kuruma**
very **totemo**; *very much* **totemo**
vest **chokki, besuto**
vet **ju-i**
video games **bideo gehmu**
video tape **bideo tehpu**
view **keshiki, nagame**
viewfinder **fainda**
villa **bessoh**
village **mura**
vinegar **su**; (vinegared food) **sunomono**
violin **baiorin**
visa **biza**
visit **hohmon**; (verb) **hohmon suru**
visitor **hohmonsha**; (tourist) **ryokoh sha**
vitamin tablet **bitaminzai**
vodka **uokkah**
voice **koe**
voicemail **boisu mehru**
VR headset **buiahru heddo setto**

W

wait (verb) **matsu**
waiter (server) **uehtah**; *waiter!* **sumimasen**
waiting room **machiai shitsu**
waitress (server) **uehtoresu**
Wales **Uehruzu**
walk (stroll) **sanpo**; (verb) **sanpo suru, aruku**; *to go for a walk* **sanpo ni iku**
wall **kabe**
wallet **saifu**
want (preference) **konomi**
want to take **noritai**
war **sensoh**
ward **byohtoh**
wardrobe **yohfuku-dansu; curohzetto**
warm (adj) **atatakai**
was: I was **watashi wa... deshita**; *he was* **kare wa... deshita**; *she was* **kanojo wa... deshita**; *it was* **sore wa... deshita**

wash basin **senmendai**

washing machine **sentaku ki**

washing powder **sentaku yoh senzai**

washing-up liquid **shokki yoh senzai**

wasp **suzume-bachi**

watch (wristwatch) **udedokei**; (verb) **miru**

water **mizu**; (onsen, cloudy, mineral-rich) **nigori yu**

waterfall **taki**; (onsen) **utase yu**

wave **nami**; (verb) **te o furu**

we **watashi tachi**

weak **yowai**

weather **tenki**

Web site **Web saito**

wedding **kekkonshiki**

Wednesday **suiyohbi**

week **shu**

welcome! **yohkoso**

well: I don't feel well **chohshi ga warui desu**

wellingtons **nagagutsu**

Welsh (adj) **uehruzu** (**no**)

went (verb, past) **ikimashita**

were: we were **watashi tachi wa... deshita**; *you were* **anata wa... deshita**; (sing. informal) **kimi wa... deshita**; *they were* **karera wa... deshita**

west **nishi**; *the West* **seiyoh**

Westerner **seiyoh jin**

Western-style (adj) **yohfuu**; (cuisine) **sehyoh ryohri**

wet (adj) **nureta**

what? **nani, nandesuka**

wheel (of vehicle) **sharin**; (steering) **handoru**

wheelchair **kurumaisu**

when? **itsu**

where? **doko**

which? (of two) **dochira**; (of more than two) **dore**

whisky **uisukih**

white (adj) **shiro**

who? **dare/donata**; (formal) *whom: with whom?* **dare/donata to**

why? **naze, dohshite**

Wi-Fi password **wai fai pasuwahdo**

wide (adj) **hiroi**

wife **okusan**; *my wife* **tsuma**

wind **kaze**

window **mado**

windscreen **furonto garasu**

wine **wain, budohshu**; (rice wine) **osake/nihon-shu**

wine list **wain risuto**

wing **tsubasa, hane**

wing mirror **saido mirah**

winter **fuyu**

with (together with) **...to issho ni**; *I'll go with you* **a nata to issho ni ikimasu**;(using) **...de**; *with a pen* **pen de**; *with sugar* **satoh iri**

without **...nashi** (**de**); *without sugar* **satoh nashide**

witness (person) **shoh nin**

woman **onna; jyoseh**

women (toilet) **fujin toire**

wood **mori, zaimoku**

wool **yohmoh**

word **kotoba**

work **shigoto**; (verb) **hataraku**; *it doesn't work* **ugokimasen**

worktop (kitchen) **chohridai**

worse **motto warui**

worst **saiaku** (**na**)

wrapping paper **tsutsumi-gami, hohsohshi**

wrap **tsutsumu**

wrist **tekubi**

write (verb) **kaku**

writing paper **binsen**

wrong (adj): *it is wrong* **machigatte imasu**

X, Y, Z

x-ray **rentogen**; *x-ray ward* **rentogen shitsu**

year **nen, toshi**

yellow (adj) **ki iro**

yen **en**

yes **hai**

yesterday **kinoh**

yet **moh**; *not yet* **mada**

yoghurt **yohguruto**

you (sing. formal) **anata**; (sing. informal) **kimi**; (plural formal) **anata-gata**; (plural informal) **kimitachi**

young (adj) **wakai**

your: your shoe(s) (formal) **anata no kutsu**; (informal) **kimi no kutsu**

yours: is this yours? (formal) **kore wa anata no desuka**; (informal) **kore, kimi no**

youth hostel **yu-su hosuteru**

zen **zen**

zen Buddhism **zenshu**

zen garden **zendera no niwa**

zip **chakku, zippah**

zoo **dohbutsuen**

The Japanese writing system

It is not as difficult to decipher the Japanese script as it may first appear. Japanese is written in three different character systems, often found within the same sentence: kanji, hiragana, and katakana. Kanji are Chinese pictograms that need to be learnt individually, while hiragana and katakana are "syllabaries", with each character representing a separate syllable. The full syllabaries are given in this section to help you work out the characters in a particular word. With time, you will be able to distinguish the three systems and become more familiar with the most common characters and words. Look back over the words and phrases in the book and see how many kanji, hiragana, and katakana characters you can identify.

Kanji

Japanese kanji ideograms – such as 車 **kuruma** (*car*) or 母 **haha** (*my mother*) – are traditional Chinese characters imported into the Japanese language. They represent an idea rather than a particular sound, and need to be learnt individually. Some kanji are simple and resemble the item they describe, like the character for people: 人 (**jin/nin**), but many are quite intricate – for example, the three characters 準備中 (**jyun bi chu**) in restaurants mean *preparation in progress*, a polite way of saying "not yet open".

Kanji characters can be combined to convey a new meaning. For example, 空港 **ku-koh** (*airport*) is a combination of two kanji characters: 空 **ku** (*sky*) and 港 **koh** (*port*). Similarly, police is written as 警察 **kehsatsu**. Adding the character 官 **kan** will give you *policeman* (警察官 **kehsatsu kan**), and adding 署 **sho** will produce *police station* (警察署 **kehsatsu sho**). Kanji characters are used for other useful signs, such as 受付 **uketsuke** (*reception*) and 窓口 **madoguchi** (*information desk*, literally *window mouth*). Most basic words referring to natural features or animals, such as tree, dog, flower, and cow, are also written in kanji, often with just a single character.

It is useful to be able to recognize the Japanese kanji characters for a hospital: 病院 **byoh-in**, literally *sick building*. The first character 病 **byoh** can also be found in other compound words such as 病気 **byoh-ki**, meaning *sickness*, and 病人 **byoh-nin**, meaning *sick person* or *patient*.

When you see price labels, you may sometimes see the kanji character 円 with the price in Western figures – for example, 299円. More typically you will see the symbol for yen (¥), with a full stop and dash after the amount meaning *and no more* – for example, ¥9,950.–

Hiragana

Hiragana forms the base for learning Japanese. The system has 46 characters, each representing a key sound or individual syllable – for example, で **de** or れ **re**. These two syllables are usually used for words with a Japanese origin and for grammatical words – for example, です **desu** (*is*) and あれ **a-re** (*that*).

Most adjectives (pp64–5) are written using a mixture of hiragana and kanji characters. For example, in 大きい **ohkih** and 美しい **utsukushih**, the first kanji character carries the core meaning – 大 (*big*), 美 (*beautiful*) – while the hiragana characters attached to the kanji are grammatical endings.

The full hiragana syllabary is shown below.

あ a	か ka	さ sa	た ta	な na
い i	き ki	し shi	ち chi	に ni
う u	く ku	す su	つ tsu	ぬ nu
え e	け ke	せ se	て te	ね ne
お o	こ ko	そ so	と to	の no

は ha	ま ma	や ya	ら ra	わ wa
ひ hi	み mi		り ri	
ふ fu	む mu	ゆ yu	る ru	
へ he	め me		れ re	
ほ ho	も mo	よ yo	ろ ro	を wo
				ん n

Katakana

The katakana system has 46 characters and is mainly used for foreign loan words, such as アメリカ **amerika** (*America*) and ケーキ **kehki** (*cake*). Some traditional Japanese words used in a business context have alternative English loan words. These imported words are written in katakana characters – for example, オーダー **ohdah** (*order*), ドキュメント **dokyumento** (*document*), and レポート **repohto** (*report*). Most Western clothing items are also written in katakana as opposed to clothes that have existed traditionally in Japan, which are written in hiragana.

The full katakana syllabary is shown below.

ア a	カ ka	サ sa	タ ta	ナ na
イ i	キ ki	シ shi	チ chi	ニ ni
ウ u	ク ku	ス su	ツ tsu	ヌ nu
エ e	ケ ke	セ se	テ te	ネ ne
オ o	コ ko	ソ so	ト to	ノ no

ハ ha	マ ma	ヤ ya	ラ ra	ワ wa
ヒ hi	ミ mi		リ ri	
フ fu	ム mu	ユ yu	ル ru	
ヘ he	メ me		レ re	
ホ ho	モ mo	ヨ yo	ロ ro	ヲ wo
				ン n

Additional marks

There are two signs (" and °) that are used to add additional sounds to the characters in the syllabaries. For example, the katakana character ヒ **hi** can become ピ **pi**, while the hiragana characters て **te** can become で **de** and ほ **ho** can become ぽ **po**.

In addition, a long dash (—) is used to lengthen katakana syllables. For example, the character テ **te** is lengthened to テ— **teh** by adding this dash, used in a word such as テーブル **tehburu** (*table*); the character ピ **pi** is lengthened to ピ— **pih**, used in a word such as コピ— **kopih** (*photocopy*).

Particles

The Japanese often end their sentences with short particles or markers that don't really change the meaning of the sentence but carry different nuances. For example, the よ **yo** marker can imply *and even* or *to be sure* and ね **ne** can mean something like *isn't that so* in words such as **desuyo** and **desune**. The question marker か **ka** is often added to the end of a sentence to form a question (pp12–13) and can be seen in words such as **desuka**. Two other particles that are commonly used are the subject markers が **ga** and は **wa**, which are placed after the subject of a sentence: subject + **ga/wa** + the rest of the sentence + **desu**.

Acknowledgments

FOURTH EDITION (2024)
For this edition, the publisher would like to thank Suefa Lee and Sarah Mathew for editorial assistance; Debjyoti Mukherjee and Sonakshi Singh for design assistance; Nunhoih Guite, Manpreet Kaur, and Deepak Negi for picture research assistance; Karen Constanti for assistance with artwork commissioning; Peter Bull Art Studio and Mark Clifton for additional illustrations; and Andiamo! Language Services Ltd for the editorial review and foreign language proofreading.

THIRD EDITION (2019)
Senior Editors Angela Gavira, Christine Stroyan; **Project Art Editor** Vanessa Marr; **Art Editor** Shreya Anand; **Editor** Kingshuk Ghoshal; **Jacket Design Development Manager** Sophia MTT; **Jacket Designer** Suhita Dharamjit; **Pre-Producer** Robert Dunn; **DTP Designer** Anita Yadav; **Producer** Jude Crozier; **Associate Publisher** Liz Wheeler; **Publishing Director** Jonathan Metcalf

FIRST EDITION (2005)
The publisher would like to thank the following for their help in the preparation of this book. In Japan: Hajime Fukase, Keihin Kyuko Bus Co., Ltd, Takao Abe, Seitoku Kinen Kaigakan, Koei drug, Ichinoyu group, East Japan Railway Company (JR), East Japan Marketing & Communications, Inc. (JR Higashi Nihon Kikaku), Kenichi Miyokawa, Naoki Ogawa, Yumiko Nagahari. In the UK: Capel Manor College, Toyota (GB), Magnet Kitchens Kentish Town, Canary Wharf plc, St. Giles College, Yo! Sushi.

Produced for Dorling Kindersley by Schermuly Design Co **Language content for Dorling Kindersley by** g-and-w publishing **Managed by** Jane Wightwick **Picture research** Hugh Schermuly, Hajime Fukase

PICTURE CREDITS

The publisher would like to thank the following for their kind permission to reproduce their photographs.

Key: a-above; b-below/bottom; c-centre; f-far; l-left; r-right; t-top

1 Dreamstime.com: Noppakun. **2 Dreamstime.com:** Peter Adams (br); Niradj (tr). **3 Dreamstime.com:** Chanchai Duangdoosan (bl); Tomo Photography (tr). **Getty Images / iStock:** E+ / visualspace (br). **Shutterstock.com:** Nishihama (tl). **8 Getty Images / iStock:** maroke (cr). **9 Getty Images / iStock:** E+ / stockstudioX (tl). **10 Getty Images:** ABSODELS / Indeed (cr). **Getty Images / iStock:** E+ / kohei_hara (bl). **11 123RF.com:** sal73it (tl). **12 Getty Images / iStock:** miya227 (cr). **13 Getty Images / iStock:** Rawpixel (br). **14 Dreamstime.com:** Syda Productions (crb). **Getty Images / iStock:** E+ / JohnnyGreig (cr); imtmphoto (br). **Shutterstock.com:** TimeImage Production (cra). **15 Getty Images / iStock:** E+ / PonyWang (cla); junce (clb); mapo (bl). **17 Getty Images:** ABSODELS / Indeed (bl). **Getty Images / iStock:** E+ / stockstudioX (ca). **18–19 Getty Images / iStock:** Visit Roemvanitch (c). **18 Dreamstime.com:** Dragan Andrii (crb). **Getty Images / iStock:** kf4851 (cb). **19 Dreamstime.com:** Pongsak Tawansaeng (c). **Getty Images / iStock:** E+ / AsiaVision (cb). **20 Getty Images / iStock:** akiyoko (ca); E+ / Synergee (crb). **21 Getty Images / iStock:** GeloKorol (clb); monzenmachi (tl). **22 Dreamstime.com:** Chatkrit Kunudom (cb); Stargatechris (crb). **Getty Images / iStock:** bonchan (bl); espion (cr). **23 Getty Images / iStock:** ahirao_photo (clb). **24 Getty Images / iStock:** E+ / yanguolin (bl); Tanya_F (cr). **25 Dreamstime.com:** Bignai (tl). **Getty Images / iStock:** E+ / kokouu (clb); PeopleImages (cla); maroke (cl); mapo (bl). **26 Dreamstime.com:** Dragan Andrii (bc/Sugar Stick). **Getty Images / iStock:** kf4851 (bc); Rawpixel (crb); Visit Roemvanitch (br). **27 Dreamstime.com:** Chatkrit Kunudom (tc). **Getty Images / iStock:** akiyoko (clb); E+ / Synergee (bc). **28 123RF.com:** Kaspars Grinvalds (crb). **Dreamstime.com:** Robert Kneschke (br). **Getty Images / iStock:** maroke (cra). **29 Getty Images / iStock:** E+ / yoshiurara (clb); Wako Megumi (bl); metamorworks (cl). **30 Dreamstime.com:** Syda Productions (crb). **31 Getty Images / iStock:** E+ / AsiaVision (cl). **32 Getty Images / iStock:** E+ / LeoPatrizi (cr). **33 Getty Images / iStock:** maroke (tl, cla, cl, clb). **34–35 Dreamstime.com:** Jiri Hera (ca). **34 Dreamstime.com:** Roman Egorov (cl). **Getty Images:** fStop / Halfdark (cr). **Shutterstock.com:** Araddara (cb). **35 Getty Images / iStock:** E+ / Anastasia Dobrusina (cb); mapo (tc); Koji_Ishii (c). **Getty Images:** Photodisc / Creative Crop (cl). **36 Dreamstime.com:** Roman Egorov (cla). **Getty Images:** Photodisc / Creative Crop (ca). **36–37 Dreamstime.com:** Jiri Hera (ca). **37 Getty Images:** fStop / Halfdark (cla). **Getty Images / iStock:** Tanya_F (bl). **38 Getty Images / iStock:** ablokhin (cr). **39 Getty Images / iStock:** bee32 (cb); Ziga Plahutar (cla). **40 Dreamstime.com:** Noppakun (cr). **Shutterstock.com:** Dragos Asaftei (bl). **41 Dreamstime.com:** Cowardlion (clb/Train); Chih Yuan Wu (clb); Tktktk (bl). **Getty Images / iStock:** E+ / xijian (cla). **42 Getty Images / iStock:** Tuayai (cr). **43 Dreamstime.com:** Sean Pavone (tl); Tktktk (cla). **Getty Images / iStock:** Eloi_Omella (cl). **Shutterstock.com:** KenSoftTH (cb). **44–45 Shutterstock.com:** Nerthuz (cla). **45 Getty Images / iStock:** Saran Hansakul (tc); shylendrahoode (ca). **46–47 Getty Images / iStock:** Tuayai (tc). **46 Dreamstime.com:** Chanchai Duangdoosan (br). **Getty Images / iStock:** tapanuth (ca). **Shutterstock.com:** Dragos Asaftei (cra); Nerthuz (tc). **47 Getty Images / iStock:** ablokhin (bl). **Shutterstock.com:** KenSoftTH (cla). **48–49 Dreamstime.com:** Cowardlion (c). **48 Alamy Stock Photo:** Shigemitsu Takahashi (br). **Dreamstime.com:** Niradj (cb/Museum); Takoyaki3 (bc).

Getty Images / iStock: Thomas Faull (cb). **49 Dreamstime.com:** A1977 (bl); Samarttiw (tl). **50 Shutterstock. com:** PR Image Factory (cb). **50-51 Dreamstime.com:** Sanga Park (c). **51 Dreamstime.com:** Kittichai Boonpong (cb); Andrey Popov (cb/Phone). **52 Alamy Stock Photo:** Stephen Fleming (cr). **53 Alamy Stock Photo:** Image Farm Inc. / James Dawson (cla/Disabled sign). **Dreamstime.com:** Inurbanspace (cla). **Getty Images / iStock:** brightstars (tl). **54 Alamy Stock Photo:** Moodboard Stock Photography (cr). **Dreamstime. com:** Fizkes (br); Geargodz (crb). **55 Dreamstime.com:** Gaid Phitthayakormsilp (tl); Sergio Delle Vedove (clb/ Ticket); Tminaz (clb/Passport). **Getty Images / iStock:** E+ / goc (clb); Nirad (cla). **Shutterstock.com:** jamesteohart (br). **56-57 Shutterstock.com:** Nerthuz (bc). **56 Alamy Stock Photo:** Shigemitsu Takahashi (tr). **Dreamstime.com:** Cowardlion (cr); Samarttiw (ca); Niradj (tc/Museum); Takoyaki3 (tc). **Getty Images / iStock:** Thomas Faull (bc). **57 Getty Images / iStock:** Ziga Plahutar (bc). **58 Dreamstime.com:** David Brooks (crb). **Getty Images / iStock:** BongkarnThanyakij (cr); E+ / zeljkosantrac (crb/Family). **Shutterstock.com:** Nishihama (cra). **59 Dreamstime.com:** Rommel Gonzalez (tl). **Getty Images / iStock:** t_kimura (clb). **60 Getty Images / iStock:** AlexandrBognat (crb); surachetsh (cb); Supawat Bursuk (bl); Yastrebinsky (crb/Bathrobe). **Shutterstock.com:** Sarymsakov Andrey (c). **61 Dreamstime.com:** Chernetskaya (cla/Soap); Sebastian Czapnik (cl). **Getty Images / iStock:** Dmytro Duda (cla); yipengge (tl). **62 Getty Images / iStock:** chuck (c). **62-63 Shutterstock.com:** elfarero (c). **63 Dreamstime.com:** Tomo Photography (tc). **Getty Images / iStock:** maroke (ca); gyro (c). **64 Getty Images / iStock:** coward_lion (c). **65 Alamy Stock Photo:** Arcaid Images / Richard Bryant (clb/Wash basin). **Dreamstime.com:** Apiwan Borrikonratchata (cla). **Shutterstock.com:** zmkstudio (clb). **66 Alamy Stock Photo:** Arcaid Images / Richard Bryant (c). **Getty Images / iStock:** chuck (cb). **66-67 Shutterstock.com:** elfarero (bc). **67 Dreamstime.com:** Goir (bc). **Shutterstock.com:** Nishihama (c). **68 Alamy Stock Photo:** CNMages (cr); Jeffrey Isaac Greenberg 10+ (ca); FoodPix (c). **Dreamstime.com:** Mathiasrhode (crb); Belinda Wu (c); Kasarp Techawongtham (cr). **69 Alamy Stock Photo:** Kristina Blokhin (clb). **Dreamstime.com:** Surya Nair (cl). **Getty Images / iStock:** nastya_ph (tl). **Shutterstock.com:** Phurinee Chinakathum (cla). **70-71 Dreamstime.com:** Phive2015 (c). **70 Dreamstime.com:** Nattawat Kaewjirasit (ca). **Getty Images / iStock:** Umesh Chandra (c). **71 Dreamstime.com:** Giovanni Seabra (tc). **Getty Images / iStock:** onurdongel (ca); Promo_Link (c). **72 Shutterstock.com:** Ned Snowman (bl). **73 Dreamstime.com:** Gerold Grotelueschen (cla/Wine). **Getty Images / iStock:** E+ / Janine Lamontagne (tl); maroke (cla); E+ / MarkSwallow (clb). **Shutterstock.com:** jennywonderland (clb/Milk). **74 Alamy Stock Photo:** Aflo Co. Ltd. / AM Corporation (c). **75 Getty Images / iStock:** leolintang (br). **76 Alamy Stock Photo:** FoodPix (br); Jeffrey Isaac Greenberg 10+ (cb). **Dreamstime.com:** Nattawat Kaewjirasit (tr); Phive2015 (cra); Mathiasrhode (cb/Market); Surya Nair (crb); Kasarp Techawongtham (bc); Belinda Wu (bc/Cake). **Getty Images / iStock:** Umesh Chandra (ca). **78 Getty Images / iStock:** DragonImages (br); E+ / eli_asenova (cr). **79 Getty Images / iStock:** Worawee Meepian (cla); Wichayada Suwanachun (tl, cl/x2). **Shutterstock.com:** Zhu Difeng (bl). **82 Dreamstime.com:** Shao-chun Wang (cr). **Getty Images / iStock:** gorodenkoff (cra); Chunyip Wong (crb). **83 Dreamstime.com:** Willy Setiadi (ca). **84-85 Getty Images / iStock:** itakayuki (c). **84 Getty Images / iStock:** mayina (bl). **85 Getty Images / iStock:** ArLawKa AungTun (ca); PeopleImages (tc); shironosov (c); fizkes (cb); takasuu (bc). **86 Getty Images / iStock:** DragonImages (br). **87 Dreamstime.com:** Belinda Wu (bl). **Getty Images / iStock:** E+ / AsiaVision (bc). **88 Getty Images / iStock:** E+ / somethingway (bc). **89 Dreamstime.com:** Amenic181 (bl). **Getty Images / iStock:** RyanKing999 (clb). **90 Dreamstime.com:** Eyewave (cb). **Getty Images / iStock:** E+ / duckycards (cra). **91 Getty Images / iStock:** kuppa_rock (cla). **92 Getty Images / iStock:** E+ / TommL (cr). **93 Dreamstime.com:** Isolateshin (cb); Jomkwan (tl). **94 Getty Images / iStock:** E+ / Morsa Images (cr); Kiwis (br). **95 Getty Images / iStock:** E+ / JohnnyGreig (tl); E+ / Nikada (clb). **96 Getty Images / iStock:** E+ / somethingway (t). **97 Alamy Stock Photo:** Aflo Co. Ltd. / AM Corporation (t). **Dreamstime.com:** Jomkwan (b). **98-99 Alamy Stock Photo:** Japan Stock Photography (c). **99 Alamy Stock Photo:** Itsik Marom (tc). **Dreamstime.com:** Laupri (ca). **Getty Images / iStock:** Artjafara (ca/Home); takasuu (tl). **100 Dreamstime. com:** Bongkochrut Rojanatreekoon (cb). **Getty Images / iStock:** sihuo0860371 (cr). **102-103 Getty Images / iStock:** Lya_Cattel (b). **102 Dreamstime.com:** Smileus (cb, cra). **Getty Images / iStock:** Antonel (cla). **103 Dreamstime.com:** Peter Adams (cla); Luminouslens (tll); Yongnian Gui (cl). **Getty Images / iStock:** k--k (cla/ Hydrangea). **105 Getty Images / iStock:** lukyeee1976 (c). **Shutterstock.com:** maroke (bl). **106-107 Getty Images / iStock:** sihuo0860371 (bc). **106 Dreamstime.com:** Bongkochrut Rojanatreekoon (bc). **107 Alamy Stock Photo:** Itsik Marom (c). **Getty Images / iStock:** Lya_Cattel (bc). **108 Getty Images / iStock:** Akhilesh Sharma (crb). **Getty Images / iStock:** Wako Megumi (crb/Stamp). **Shutterstock.com:** PaulSat (cr). **109 Getty Images / iStock:** mediaphotos (cla). **110 Getty Images / iStock:** E+ / gahsoon (cr). **111 Dreamstime.com:** Diego Vito Cervo (tl). **Shutterstock.com:** yoshi0511 (clb). **112 Dreamstime.com:** Fukamiyoga (cr). **Getty Images / iStock:** E+ / BraunS (bl). **113 Dreamstime.com:** Dark1elf (tl). **Getty Images / iStock:** Bim (bl); imtmphoto (cl); SunnyVMD (clb). **114 Dreamstime.com:** Amsis1 (br); Brett Critchley (crb); Rodworksgh (crb/Money). **Getty Images / iStock:** E+ / South_agency (cr). **115 Alamy Stock Photo:** Aflo Co., Ltd. (cl). **116 Dreamstime.com:** Diego Vito Cervo (c); Akhilesh Sharma (crb). **Getty Images / iStock:** mediaphotos (br); Wako Megumi (cb/ Stamp). **Shutterstock.com:** PaulSat (cb). **118-119 Getty Images / iStock:** E+ / tanukiphoto (c). **119 Getty Images / iStock:** E+ / JGalione (cb). **120 Dreamstime.com:** Okea (br); Sergeyoch (cb); Volkop (crb/Racket); Pincarel (crb/Golfball). **Getty Images / iStock:** E+ / visualspace (bc). **Shutterstock.com:** Mirko Kuzmanovic (cr). **121 Getty Images / iStock:** E+ / Yagi-Studio (cla). **122-123 Getty Images / iStock:** Kiwis (c). **123 Dreamstime. com:** Akiyoko74 (ca). **124 Dreamstime.com:** Mikhail Kokhanchikov (cb/Football); Volkop (cb/Racket); Sergeyoch (cb). **Getty Images / iStock:** E+ / visualspace (br). **Shutterstock.com:** Mirko Kuzmanovic (br). **126 Alamy Stock Photo:** Japan Stock Photography (c). **127 Dreamstime.com:** Syda Productions (tr). **Getty Images / iStock:** E+ / somethingway (cr)

All other images © Dorling Kindersley Limited